ST. JOHN

TRAVEL GUIDE

2024-2025

Your Complete insider manual to exploring the best of US virgin Islands in the Carribean.

St john usvi

Copyright © 2024 [Jack Armstrong]

St john usvi

TABLE OF CONTENTS

Introduction 7

Overview of St. John, U.S. Virgin Islands 7

Brief History and Culture 9

Ideal Times to Visit 12

Chapter 1. Planning Your Trip 16

Entry requirements and travel documents 16

Health and Safety Considerations 19

Currency, Language, and Local Etiquette 23

Packing Tips for St. John 28

Chapter 2. Getting There 33

How to Reach St. John: Flights and Ferries 33

Transportation Options on the Island 37

Car Rentals and Driving Tips 42

Chapter 3. Accommodations 48

Hotels and resorts 48

Vacation rentals and villas 53

Chapter 4. Cuisine and Dining 58

3

Must-Try Dishes and Drinks 58

Top restaurants and eateries 64

Chapter 5. Must-See Attractions............................ 69

Virgin Islands National Park 69

Trunk Bay and the Underwater Snorkel Trail 79

Annaberg Plantation Ruins................................... 81

Cinnamon Bay and Water Sports 86

Chapter 6. Activities and Adventures.................... 93

Snorkeling and Diving Hotspots 93

Hiking Trails and Nature Walks........................... 99

Boating, Sailing, and Kayaking........................... 105

Shopping and Local Markets............................... 111

Chapter 7. Suggested Itineraries.......................... 118

Family-Friendly Itinerary 118

Adventure Seekers Itinerary 126

Cultural and Historical Itinerary......................... 135

Chapter 8. Practical Information........................ 144

Emergency Contacts and Medical Services 144

St john usvi

Internet and Mobile Connectivity........................ 147

Tipping and Service Charges............................ 149

Conclusion **153**

St john usvi

Introduction

Overview of St. John, U.S. Virgin Islands

Imagine an island where the rhythm of the waves gently guides your days, where the sun kisses your skin with a golden warmth, and where every corner holds a story waiting to be told. This is St. John, the jewel of the U.S. Virgin Islands, a place where nature and serenity blend into a perfect escape from the everyday.

St. John is the smallest of the three main U.S. Virgin Islands, but what it lacks in size, it more than makes up for in beauty and charm. With over two-thirds of the island protected as part of Virgin Islands National Park, St. John remains a pristine paradise, untouched by the hustle and bustle of modern life. Here, lush green hills tumble into turquoise waters, and secluded coves invite you to dive into their clear, warm embrace.

But St. John is more than just breathtaking landscapes; it's a place rich in history and culture. The island's past is etched into the ruins of sugar plantations and the vibrant traditions of its people. As you explore, you'll find traces of a time when the island was a hub of sugar production, and you'll hear stories passed down through generations, stories that speak of resilience, community, and a deep connection to the land.

For those seeking adventure, St. John offers endless opportunities to explore, from snorkeling through coral reefs teeming with life to hiking trails that wind through dense forests and lead to panoramic vistas. For those looking to unwind, the island's peaceful beaches, like Trunk Bay and Cinnamon Bay, provide the perfect setting for relaxation, where the only sounds are the rustling of palm trees and the gentle lapping of waves.

But perhaps the true magic of St. John lies in its ability to make you feel at home, no matter how far you've traveled to get there. The locals, with their warm smiles and welcoming spirit, make you feel like you've been invited into their world, a world where the pace of life is slow, the beauty is boundless, and every moment is savored.

Whether you're seeking adventure, relaxation, or a bit of both, St. John, U.S. Virgin Islands, offers a sanctuary where you can reconnect with nature, with loved ones, and with yourself. It's not just a destination; it's a place that touches your soul and leaves you longing to return, long after the sand has washed from your feet.

Brief History and Culture

St. John's history is a tapestry woven with threads of resilience, struggle, and the enduring spirit of its people. Long before the arrival of European settlers, the island was home to the Taíno people, who lived in harmony with the land, drawing sustenance from the sea and the fertile soil. Their legacy still whispers through the petroglyphs etched into the rocks, silent yet powerful reminders of a time when the island was a sacred place of life and reverence.

In the early 18th century, everything changed with the arrival of Danish settlers. The island's lush terrain was quickly transformed into sprawling sugar plantations, worked by the hands of enslaved Africans brought across the ocean. These plantations were the heart of St. John's economy, but they were also the site of unimaginable hardship and suffering. Yet even in the darkest of times, the human spirit proved unbreakable. The enslaved people of St. John rose up in a historic revolt in 1733, one of the earliest and most significant rebellions in the Caribbean. Their fight for freedom is a testament to their courage and unyielding desire for justice, a story of defiance that echoes through the ages.

The abolition of slavery in 1848 marked a new chapter for St. John, as the island's freed people began to reclaim their lives and their land. The remnants of the old plantations, like the hauntingly beautiful ruins of Annaberg, stand today as monuments to both a painful past and a hopeful future. They are places of reflection, where visitors can honor the resilience of those who came before and the enduring strength of the island's culture.

St. John's culture is a vibrant blend of African, European, and indigenous influences, a mosaic of traditions that have shaped the island's identity. This cultural richness is celebrated in everything from the vibrant colors of local art to the infectious rhythms of calypso and reggae music that fill the air during festivals. The island's people, known for their warmth and hospitality, carry forward the traditions of their ancestors with pride, ensuring that the stories, songs, and customs of St. John continue to thrive.

Today, St. John is a place where history is not just remembered but lived. The island's culture is woven into the fabric of everyday life, from the flavors of traditional dishes like fish and fungi to the joy of a community gathering on the beach. It's a place where the past is honored, the present is cherished, and the future is embraced with open arms.

As you explore St. John, you'll feel the pulse of its history and the pride of its people in every corner. It's a story of survival, of adaptation, and of a culture that, like the island itself, is both resilient and beautiful.

Ideal Times to Visit

Choosing the perfect time to visit St. John is like selecting the best moment to unwrap a gift—no matter when you arrive, you're sure to find something special waiting for you. Yet, each season brings its own magic to the island, shaping your experience in unique and unforgettable ways.

St john usvi

Winter (December to April) is when St. John truly shines. The air is filled with a crisp freshness, the sun is warm but not overbearing, and the skies are an endless stretch of deep blue. This is the island's peak season, a time when travelers from around the world flock to its shores in search of an escape from the cold. During these months, the island is alive with energy, from the bustling streets of Cruz Bay to the vibrant beaches where the days are spent snorkeling, sunbathing, and soaking in the beauty of it all. The trade winds dance across the waters, making the waves sparkle like diamonds, and the sunsets—oh, the sunsets—paint the sky with hues that can only be described as pure poetry.

As spring gives way to **Summer (May to August),** the island takes on a slower, more intimate pace. The crowds thin, leaving you with a sense of having St. John all to yourself. The days grow longer, the beaches quieter, and the island's lush greenery reaches its peak. This is the time for those who seek a deeper connection with nature, for explorers who wish to hike

13

the trails of Virgin Islands National Park in solitude or find their own hidden cove along the shoreline. The waters are calm, warm, and inviting, perfect for a lazy day of swimming or paddleboarding in the serene embrace of the Caribbean Sea.

Then comes **Autumn (September to November),** a time of renewal and tranquility. This is the island's quietest season, often referred to as the off-season. While there is a chance of tropical storms, the rewards for those who visit are plentiful. The island is lush from the rains, the beaches are practically deserted, and there's a sense of peace that blankets the land. It's a time for introspection, for finding beauty in the simplicity of a deserted beach, or for witnessing the resilience of nature as the island bounces back from the summer rains. It's a season of reflection, where the beauty of St. John feels like a secret shared just between you and the island itself.

St john usvi

No matter when you choose to visit, St. John welcomes you with open arms and an open heart. Each season offers a different lens through which to view the island's beauty, whether it's the lively pulse of winter, the relaxed vibe of summer, or the serene calm of autumn. The best time to visit? It's whenever your heart is ready to be captivated by the magic of St. John.

Chapter 1. Planning Your Trip

Entry requirements and travel documents

As of late 2024, entry requirements and travel documents for tourists visiting St. John, U.S. Virgin Islands (USVI), depend on the traveler's citizenship and the nature of their visit.

U.S. Citizens:

Since the U.S. Virgin Islands are a U.S. territory, U.S. citizens do not need a passport to enter St. John. Travelers can enter with a government-issued photo ID, such as a driver's license. However, having a passport is recommended, especially if travel plans include visits to nearby international destinations like the British Virgin Islands.

For minors under 18 traveling without both parents, a notarized letter of consent from the non-accompanying parent(s) is advisable, although not always required.

Non-U.S. Citizens:

Non-U.S. citizens, including permanent residents (Green Card holders), must have a valid passport to enter St. John. Depending on their nationality, they may also need a U.S. visa. Citizens from countries that participate in the Visa Waiver Program (VWP) can enter without a visa but must have an approved Electronic System for Travel Authorization (ESTA). Travelers from non-VWP countries must obtain a B-1/B-2 tourist visa before traveling.

COVID-19 Requirements:

As of mid-2024, there are no COVID-19 testing or vaccination requirements to enter the U.S. Virgin Islands. However, travelers are encouraged to stay informed about any changes that may arise due to new health advisories.

Customs and Immigration:

Upon arrival in St. John, U.S. citizens do not go through customs if traveling directly from the U.S. mainland. However, when returning to the mainland U.S., all travelers must clear customs, and U.S. citizens must present proof of citizenship (passport, passport card, or enhanced driver's license).

Additional Considerations:

Travel insurance is recommended for all travelers, covering health, travel delays, and potential cancellations. Also, travelers planning extended stays or those bringing pets should check for additional regulations and permits.

All the same, U.S. citizens enjoy simplified entry to St. John, needing only a photo ID, while non-U.S. citizens must ensure they have the correct visa or ESTA approval. Always check the latest travel advisories before your trip.

Health and Safety Considerations

As you prepare for your journey to St. John, it's natural to feel a mix of excitement and anticipation. Amidst the daydreams of sun-soaked beaches and crystal-clear waters, it's also important to consider the well-being of you and your loved ones. St. John may be a paradise, but taking a few simple precautions will ensure that your trip is as safe and enjoyable as possible.

Health Precautions

St. John is a relatively safe destination in terms of health, but there are a few things to keep in mind. The island's tropical climate means you'll be spending a lot of time in the sun, so protecting yourself from sunburn and heat exhaustion is essential. Be sure to pack plenty of sunscreen, preferably reef-safe to protect the island's delicate marine ecosystems, and reapply it often, especially after swimming. Wearing a wide-brimmed hat and lightweight, protective clothing can also help shield you from the sun's rays.

Mosquitoes are a part of island life, especially in the early morning and evening hours. While the risk of mosquito-borne illnesses like dengue and Zika is low, it's still wise to use insect repellent and wear long sleeves and pants when possible. If you're traveling with children or anyone with specific health concerns, it's a good idea to consult with your doctor before the trip to ensure you have everything you need to stay healthy.

Safety on the Water

St. John's waters are a dream come true for swimmers, snorkelers, and boaters, but they also deserve respect. Always be aware of your surroundings, especially when snorkeling or swimming. Strong currents can occur in certain areas, so stick to recommended spots like Trunk Bay or Cinnamon Bay, where conditions are generally safe and lifeguards are on duty.

If you plan to explore the island by boat or kayak, be sure to wear life jackets and follow local guidelines. The beauty of the ocean can sometimes mask its power, so it's important to stay cautious and prepared.

General Safety Tips

St. John is known for its friendly and welcoming atmosphere, and crime rates are low. However, as with any travel destination, it's wise to stay alert and take basic precautions. Keep your belongings secure, avoid leaving valuables unattended on the beach, and be mindful of your surroundings, especially in less populated areas.

When hiking, stick to well-marked trails and carry plenty of water, especially in the warmer months. The island's rugged terrain is part of its charm, but it also means that it's easy to get dehydrated or disoriented if you're not prepared. Let someone know your plans before heading out on longer hikes, and consider hiring a local guide if you're unfamiliar with the area.

Medical Facilities

While St. John is a small island, it's reassuring to know that medical care is available if needed. The Myrah Keating Smith Community Health Center in Cruz Bay provides basic medical services, and more comprehensive care can be accessed via a short ferry ride to St. Thomas. If you have any specific medical conditions or are traveling with children, it's a good idea to bring a copy of your medical records and any necessary medications, as pharmacies on the island may have limited supplies.

In case of an emergency, dial 911 for immediate assistance. The island's emergency responders are trained and equipped to handle a variety of situations, ensuring that you and your loved ones are in good hands.

By taking a few moments to consider these health and safety tips, you're not just preparing for your trip— you're ensuring that your time on St. John will be filled with nothing but joy, wonder, and peace of mind. After all, the goal is to return home with memories of a paradise that cared for you as much as you cared for it.

Currency, Language, and Local Etiquette

As you prepare to embrace the beauty and tranquility of St. John, understanding the island's currency, language, and local etiquette will help you feel more connected to the heart and soul of this Caribbean paradise. These small details, though often overlooked, can enhance your experience, making your interactions more meaningful and your stay more comfortable.

Currency

In St. John, the currency is as familiar as the warm breeze that greets you upon arrival: the U.S. Dollar (USD). For American visitors, this means there's no need to worry about exchange rates or converting your money. Whether you're buying a handcrafted souvenir from a local artisan, enjoying a meal at a beachfront restaurant, or tipping your guide after an unforgettable tour, the ease of using U.S. dollars adds to the island's welcoming vibe.

While most businesses accept credit and debit cards, it's always a good idea to carry some cash, especially if you plan to explore the island's more remote areas or visit local markets and smaller establishments. ATMs are available in Cruz Bay, the island's main town, but having cash on hand ensures you're prepared for those spontaneous moments when you want to support a local vendor or tip generously after a day of exceptional service.

Language

The official language of St. John is English, making communication with locals and fellow travelers a breeze. Yet, beyond the words themselves, there's a rhythm and melody to the way English is spoken here, a reflection of the island's rich cultural tapestry. You might hear phrases infused with Caribbean flair or the

St john usvi

lilting cadence of Virgin Islands Creole, a testament to the island's history and the diverse influences that have shaped its culture.

Don't be surprised if a simple greeting turns into a warm and friendly conversation. The people of St. John are known for their openness and hospitality, and they appreciate when visitors take the time to exchange a few words, ask about their day, or share a smile. Even if you're just asking for directions or ordering a meal, the island's laid-back atmosphere invites you to slow down, engage, and savor each interaction.

Local Etiquette

Understanding and respecting local etiquette is key to truly immersing yourself in the culture of St. John. The island's pace of life is relaxed, and there's a strong emphasis on community, kindness, and mutual respect. Here are a few tips to help you navigate the social landscape with grace:

St john usvi

- Greetings Matter: In St. John, taking the time to greet someone before jumping into a conversation is important. Whether you're entering a shop, boarding a ferry, or simply passing someone on a hiking trail, a friendly "Good morning" or "Good afternoon" is always appreciated.

- Respect for Nature: The island's natural beauty is its most precious asset, and locals are deeply committed to preserving it. When visiting beaches, hiking trails, or snorkeling spots, be mindful of your impact. Avoid littering, respect wildlife, and follow guidelines to protect coral reefs and other fragile ecosystems.

- Tipping: Tipping is customary in St. John and is a way to show appreciation for good service. In restaurants, a tip of 15-20% is standard. For taxi drivers, guides, and hotel staff, a tip of a few dollars is appropriate, depending on the service provided. Remember, a little extra kindness goes a long way in creating positive connections with the people you meet.

- Dress Code: While beachwear is perfect for the sand and surf, it's considered respectful to cover up when you're in town or at restaurants. Casual, lightweight clothing is the norm, but throwing on a sundress or a shirt and shorts when leaving the beach shows respect for local customs.

As you journey through St. John, you'll find that the island's currency, language, and etiquette all contribute to a sense of belonging—a feeling that you're not just a visitor but a welcomed guest in a place that's proud to share its traditions, stories, and natural wonders with you. By embracing these aspects of island life, you'll deepen your connection to St. John and create memories that feel as rich and meaningful as the island itself.

Packing Tips for St. John

Packing for St. John is more than just preparing for a trip; it's the beginning of your adventure, a chance to imagine the warm sand beneath your feet, the vibrant colors of the island, and the gentle sway of palm trees in the breeze. With every item you place in your suitcase, you're laying the foundation for days filled with exploration, relaxation, and the kind of memories that will linger long after you've returned home.

Essentials for the Tropical Climate

St. John's tropical climate is a dream, but it also calls for thoughtful packing. Lightweight, breathable clothing is your best friend here. Think airy cotton dresses, comfortable shorts, and loose-fitting shirts that will keep you cool during your island adventures. Don't forget a wide-brimmed hat to shield your face from the sun, and a pair of UV-protective sunglasses to keep your eyes comfortable as you take in the dazzling scenery.

When it comes to footwear, pack a pair of sturdy sandals or flip-flops for strolling through Cruz Bay and the beaches, and a pair of comfortable hiking shoes if you plan to explore the island's lush trails. The rugged terrain of the Virgin Islands National Park is best experienced with proper support, so make sure your shoes are up to the task.

Sun Protection

The Caribbean sun is as powerful as it is inviting, so packing sun protection is crucial. Along with sunscreen—preferably reef-safe to protect the delicate marine life—consider bringing a rash guard or long-sleeve swim shirt for extra coverage while snorkeling or swimming. After all, you want to return home with memories of the sun, not sunburn.

Swimwear

St. John is a paradise of turquoise waters and endless beaches, so packing multiple swimsuits is a must.

Whether you're diving into the waves at Trunk Bay or lounging by the pool, you'll want to have options. A cover-up is also handy for those moments when you're transitioning from the beach to a casual lunch or a stroll through town.

Adventure Gear

If your plans include snorkeling, consider bringing your own gear—mask, snorkel, and fins—so you can explore the underwater wonders of St. John whenever the mood strikes. While rental options are available on the island, having your own gear ensures a perfect fit and lets you dive into the crystal-clear waters at a moment's notice. For hikers, a daypack filled with water, snacks, and a map of the island's trails will prepare you for a day of adventure in the wild beauty of the Virgin Islands National Park.

Insect Repellent and First-Aid

Mosquitoes and other insects are part of the tropical experience, especially during the early morning and evening hours. Packing insect repellent will help keep these tiny nuisances at bay, allowing you to enjoy the island's natural beauty without distraction. It's also a good idea to bring a basic first-aid kit with band-aids, antiseptic wipes, and any personal medications you may need. While St. John is a safe destination, it's always comforting to have these essentials on hand.

Reusable Water Bottle

Staying hydrated is key to enjoying your time on St. John, especially under the tropical sun. A reusable water bottle is not only eco-friendly but also a practical way to ensure you're never far from a refreshing drink. Many beaches and hiking trails don't have easy access to water, so having your bottle filled and ready will keep you energized throughout the day.

Packing Light and Smart

Remember, St. John is all about relaxation and simplicity, so there's no need to overpack. The island's casual atmosphere means you can leave the fancy outfits at home and focus on comfort and practicality. If you find you've forgotten something, the island's shops and boutiques offer everything from beachwear to sunscreen, ensuring you're well-equipped no matter what.

As you close your suitcase, you're not just packing for a trip—you're preparing for moments that will stay with you forever. The gentle lapping of the waves, the warmth of the sun on your skin, the laughter shared with loved ones—every item you pack is a step closer to experiencing the magic of St. John. So pack with intention, with excitement, and with the knowledge that what awaits you is more than just a destination—it's a paradise that's ready to welcome you with open arms.

Chapter 2. Getting There

How to Reach St. John: Flights and Ferries

Reaching St. John is like embarking on a journey to a hidden treasure, where the path is as enchanting as the destination itself. The anticipation builds with every mile, every wave, every breeze that whispers of the paradise waiting just beyond the horizon. Getting to this island gem involves a blend of sky and sea, each step bringing you closer to the tranquil shores that will soon feel like home.

Flights to St. Thomas

Your journey to St. John begins with a flight to Cyril E. King Airport (STT) on the neighboring island of St. Thomas, the gateway to the U.S. Virgin Islands. As your plane descends, you'll catch glimpses of the sparkling Caribbean Sea, dotted with emerald islands—a view that will stir your excitement for the adventures ahead. This airport is well-connected, with direct flights from major U.S. cities such as Miami, Atlanta, New York, and Charlotte. Whether you're traveling from near or far, the flight to St. Thomas is the first step in leaving the hustle of the world behind.

From St. Thomas to St. John: The Ferry Ride

Once you've landed on St. Thomas, the final leg of your journey to St. John begins—an experience that's as much a part of the adventure as the destination itself. To reach St. John, you'll need to take a ferry from one of two locations on St. Thomas: either from the bustling Charlotte Amalie or from the more tranquil Red Hook.

- Red Hook to Cruz Bay: The most popular and frequent ferry route departs from Red Hook, located on the eastern tip of St. Thomas. After a scenic 30-minute taxi ride from the airport, you'll arrive at the Red Hook ferry terminal. As you board the ferry, you'll feel the ocean breeze and hear the gentle rhythm of the waves. The ferry ride to Cruz Bay, St. John's main town, takes about 20 minutes—a short journey that offers stunning views of the surrounding islands and the turquoise waters that separate them. The excitement builds as St. John's lush hills and inviting shores come into focus, welcoming you to a world of natural beauty and serenity.

- Charlotte Amalie to Cruz Bay: Alternatively, you can catch a ferry from Charlotte Amalie, the capital of St. Thomas. This ferry route is slightly longer, about 45 minutes, but offers the convenience of departing closer to the airport. The ride gives you a chance to relax after your flight and take in the breathtaking views as you sail through the Caribbean Sea. It's a peaceful transition from the busy port of Charlotte Amalie to the laid-back charm of Cruz Bay, where your St. John adventure truly begins.

Arriving in St. John

As the ferry docks in Cruz Bay, you'll step off the boat and into a world that feels worlds away from the everyday. The vibrant colors of the island—the green of the hills, the blue of the sea, the bright hues of the buildings—welcome you with open arms. The air is filled with the scent of saltwater and tropical flowers, and the sounds of island life—laughter, music, and the gentle sway of the palm trees—begin to weave themselves into your heart.

From here, the island is yours to explore. Whether you're heading to your accommodations, ready to dip your toes in the sand, or eager to start your adventure, the journey to St. John is a memory in itself—a blend of anticipation, beauty, and the promise of unforgettable experiences. The path to paradise may have involved flights and ferries, but now that you've arrived, you'll find that the journey was worth every moment.

St john usvi

Transportation Options on the Island

Once you've arrived on the shores of St. John, a new kind of journey begins—one that's slower, richer, and filled with moments that encourage you to savor the beauty around every bend. The island may be small, but it offers a variety of transportation options that allow you to explore its hidden gems, whether you're in the mood for adventure or simply wish to wander at your own pace.

Rental Cars: Freedom to Explore

For those who want to truly immerse themselves in the island's natural beauty, renting a car is the most convenient way to get around. St. John's winding roads, framed by lush greenery and offering glimpses of the azure sea, are a joy to navigate. A rental car gives you the freedom to explore every corner of the island—from the popular beaches like Trunk Bay and Cinnamon Bay to the secluded coves that feel like your own private paradise.

Driving on St. John is an experience in itself. The island's roads can be steep and narrow, and you'll be driving on the left side—a reminder of its British colonial history. But don't let that intimidate you; driving here is part of the adventure, and the pace is as laid-back as the island itself. Jeep rentals are particularly popular, as their sturdy build is perfect for tackling the island's terrain, especially if you plan to explore the more rugged areas like Coral Bay or the North Shore Road.

Taxis: Convenience and Local Knowledge

If you prefer to leave the driving to someone else, St. John's taxis are a reliable and easy way to get around. The island's taxis are often open-air safari-style vehicles, offering a breezy ride with panoramic views of the landscape. Taxi drivers on St. John are not just chauffeurs—they're locals with a wealth of knowledge about the island's history, culture, and hidden spots. A ride with them can turn into an impromptu tour, filled with stories and insights that only a local could share.

Taxis are readily available in Cruz Bay and at popular beaches, and they operate on fixed rates depending on your destination. While this option may be less flexible than renting a car, it's perfect for those who want to relax and enjoy the ride without worrying about navigating the island's roads.

Public Transportation: The Vitran Bus

For a truly local experience, consider taking the Vitran bus, St. John's public transportation system. The bus route runs from Cruz Bay to Coral Bay and offers a budget-friendly way to explore the island. The Vitran bus may not be the fastest mode of transportation, and its schedule can be a bit unpredictable, but it's a great option for those who want to see the island through the eyes of its residents.

Riding the Vitran bus is an opportunity to slow down and connect with the rhythm of daily life on St. John. As you travel between the island's towns and beaches, you'll be surrounded by locals going about their day, offering a glimpse into the authentic, everyday life of the island.

Biking and Walking: Embrace the Island's Pace

For the active traveler, biking or walking around St. John is a rewarding way to explore at your own pace. The island's compact size and stunning scenery make it ideal for those who want to soak in every detail of their surroundings. Cruz Bay and Coral Bay are both walkable, with plenty of shops, restaurants, and beaches within easy reach.

Biking offers a similar sense of freedom, allowing you to cover more ground while still staying connected to the island's natural beauty. However, keep in mind that St. John's roads can be hilly and challenging, so this option is best for those who are comfortable with more strenuous rides.

St john usvi

Water Taxis and Boat Rentals: Explore the Sea

St. John's beauty isn't limited to its land; the surrounding waters are just as enchanting. Water taxis and boat rentals offer a unique perspective, allowing you to explore the island from the sea. Whether you're heading to a nearby island, such as Jost Van Dyke or Tortola, or simply want to experience the thrill of gliding across the Caribbean, these options add an extra layer of adventure to your trip.

Water taxis are available for trips between the islands, and boat rentals, complete with a captain if you wish, give you the freedom to chart your own course. Imagine anchoring in a secluded bay, diving into the crystal-clear waters, and feeling the sun warm your skin as you drift in paradise.

No matter how you choose to get around, transportation on St. John isn't just about getting from point A to point B—it's about embracing the journey, allowing yourself to be guided by the island's rhythm, and finding joy in every mile, every turn, every wave. Here, the road is part of the experience, and each mode of transport offers a different way to connect with the island's soul.

Car Rentals and Driving Tips

Renting a car on St. John is more than just a way to get from place to place—it's your ticket to freedom, your invitation to explore the island's winding roads and hidden treasures at your own pace. With a set of keys in hand and the open road before you, every turn becomes an opportunity to discover something new, something breathtaking, something that will make your heart skip a beat.

Choosing the Right Rental

When it comes to car rentals on St. John, the most popular choice is a Jeep or another type of 4x4 vehicle. The island's terrain can be challenging, with steep hills, narrow roads, and the occasional unpaved path leading to a secluded beach or a panoramic overlook. A Jeep offers the perfect balance of comfort and capability, allowing you to navigate these roads with ease while also providing that classic island vibe.

Several rental companies operate out of Cruz Bay, the main town where the ferry docks. It's a good idea to book your rental in advance, especially during the high season, to ensure you get the vehicle that best suits your needs. Whether you're planning to spend your days exploring the Virgin Islands National Park, hopping from beach to beach, or simply cruising around taking in the views, having your own wheels gives you the flexibility to create your own adventure.

Driving on the Left

One of the most important things to remember when driving on St. John is that vehicles drive on the left side of the road—a legacy of the island's British colonial past. It might take a little time to get used to, especially if you're accustomed to driving on the right, but most visitors find it easier than expected. The island's roads are not heavily trafficked, and the pace is relaxed, giving you time to adjust and enjoy the experience.

As you navigate the island, you'll find that many of the roads are narrow and winding, with sharp turns and steep inclines. Take your time, especially on the hilly sections, and don't be afraid to use your horn gently to alert other drivers when approaching a blind corner. The island's laid-back atmosphere extends to the roads, so there's no rush—just enjoy the ride.

Parking in St. John

Parking in St. John can be an adventure of its own, particularly in the popular areas of Cruz Bay and at the island's most frequented beaches. Cruz Bay has several parking lots and street parking options, but spaces can fill up quickly, especially during peak times. Many restaurants and shops in Cruz Bay offer

SoncilSubstances

St john usvi

parking validation if you dine or shop with them, so keep an eye out for those options.

When visiting the beaches, you'll find parking areas at the major spots like Trunk Bay and Cinnamon Bay, though these can also fill up during the day. Arriving early is often the best strategy to secure a good spot. For more secluded beaches, parking might involve pulling over on the side of the road and walking a short distance, adding a touch of adventure to your beach day.

Fueling Up

There are only a few gas stations on St. John, so it's wise to keep an eye on your fuel gauge, especially if you're planning to explore the more remote parts of the island. Gasoline is typically more expensive here than on the mainland U.S., reflecting the cost of importing fuel to the island. Despite the higher prices, a full tank ensures you're ready to explore without any interruptions.

45

Island Driving Etiquette

Driving on St. John is about more than just following the rules of the road—it's about embracing the island's culture and pace. Islanders often wave to each other as they pass on the road, a simple gesture that reflects the warmth and friendliness of the community. When you see a raised hand, feel free to return the wave—it's a small but meaningful way to connect with the island's spirit.

It's also common to encounter donkeys, goats, or other wildlife on the road, particularly in the more rural areas. These moments are a reminder that you're in a place where nature reigns supreme, so slow down, take a breath, and enjoy the sight of these animals living their best island life.

St john usvi

Safety Tips

While St. John is generally a safe place to drive, it's important to remain cautious, especially on unfamiliar roads. Always wear your seatbelt, and avoid using your phone while driving. The island's roads can be challenging, but with a bit of patience and care, you'll find that getting around is a rewarding part of your St. John experience.

As you drive through St. John, you'll quickly realize that the journey is just as beautiful as the destination. The views from the road—the lush green hills, the sparkling blue sea, the vibrant tropical flowers—are a constant reminder that you're in a place where every moment is meant to be savored. So roll down the windows, feel the warm breeze on your face, and let the island guide you on a journey you'll never forget.

Chapter 3. Accommodations

Hotels and resorts

Here's an up-to-date information on some of the best hotels and resorts in St. John, USVI:

1. Caneel Bay Resort

Address: 10 Caneel Bay, St John, VI 00831, USVI

Phone: +1 340-776-6111

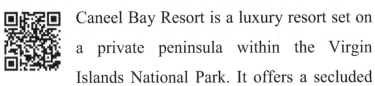 Caneel Bay Resort is a luxury resort set on a private peninsula within the Virgin Islands National Park. It offers a secluded and serene experience with access to seven pristine white-sand beaches. The resort provides complimentary water sports, a fitness center, and a pool. It's a fantastic spot for those looking for an upscale, nature-oriented retreat.

Unique Feature: The resort's location within a national park and its access to seven different beaches.

Price Range: Approximately $800 to $1,500 per night.

St john usvi

Opening Hours: Open year-round, 24/7.

2. The Westin St. John Resort & Villas

Address: 300B Chocolate Hole, Great Cruz Bay, St John, VI 00830, USVI

Phone: +1 340-693-8000

 Located on Great Cruz Bay, this family-friendly resort offers a range of accommodations, from guest rooms to villas. The Westin St. John features a large pool, multiple dining options, a spa, and a kids' club. The beachfront location makes it ideal for swimming, snorkeling, and other water activities.

Unique Feature: The resort's extensive family-friendly amenities, including a kids' club and easy access to water sports.

Price Range: $500 to $1,200 per night.

Opening Hours: Open year-round, 24/7.

St john usvi

3. Gallows Point Resort

Address: 3 AAA Gallows Point Road, Cruz Bay, St John, VI 00831, USVI

Phone: +1 340-776-6434

This condo-style resort is located on a peninsula near Cruz Bay, offering panoramic views of the harbor. Gallows Point Resort has an outdoor pool, on-site dining, and direct access to a coral reef for snorkeling. Each unit includes a full kitchen, making it a convenient choice for longer stays.

Unique Feature: The direct access to snorkeling and the beautiful harbor views.

Price Range: $450 to $900 per night.

Opening Hours: Open year-round, 24/7.

4. Lovango Resort + Beach Club

Address: Lovango Cay, St John, USVI

Phone: +1 340-693-8000

 Located on a private island just off the coast of St. John, Lovango Resort offers luxurious accommodations with stunning ocean views. The resort features an infinity pool, waterfront dining, and various nature-inspired activities like snorkeling and hiking.

Unique Feature: The private island setting and exclusive access via a 10-minute boat ride from St. John.

Price Range: $1,000 to $2,500 per night.

Opening Hours: Open year-round, 24/7.

5. Cruz Bay Boutique Hotel

Address: 74-2 Cruz Bay Town, St John, VI 00830, USVI

Phone: +1 340-642-1702

A charming and intimate hotel located in the heart of Cruz Bay, just steps from the ferry dock and Virgin Islands National Park. This boutique hotel offers cozy rooms with modern amenities, including air conditioning and flat-screen TVs. It's a great option for travelers looking for a central location.

Unique Feature: Its prime location in the heart of Cruz Bay, within walking distance of shops, restaurants, and the beach.

Price Range: $200 to $400 per night.

Opening Hours: Open year-round, 24/7.

These options offer a variety of experiences, from luxury and seclusion to more budget-friendly, centrally located

Vacation rentals and villas

Here are some top vacation rentals and villas in St. John, USVI, with all the details you will need:

1. **La Bella Villa**

Address: Coral Bay, St. John, USVI

Phone: (340) 7762739

La Bella Villa offers a serene escape with stunning views of Coral Bay and Bordeaux Mountain. The villa features 2 bedrooms, 2 baths, a fully equipped kitchen, and a large deck that provides the perfect space to relax and take in the surroundings. This villa is ideal for those looking to immerse themselves in the natural beauty of St. John while enjoying modern comforts.

Unique Feature: Spectacular views of Coral Bay and Bordeaux Mountain from a fabulous new pool and deck area.

Price Range: $350 - $600 per night

St john usvi

Opening/Closing Hours: Check-in at 3 PM, Check-out at 10 AM

2. Island Breeze Villa

Address: Coral Bay, St. John, USVI

Phone: (340) 776-2739

 Island Breeze Villa is a private 3-bedroom, 3-bathroom villa located at the end of a cul-de-sac in Coral Bay. The villa features an open layout with vaulted cypress ceilings, a gourmet kitchen, and a spacious living area. Outside, guests can enjoy the private pool, surrounded by lush tropical gardens, making it a perfect retreat for families or groups.

Unique Feature: Private and gated entry ensures utmost privacy and security.

Price Range: $400 - $750 per night

Opening/Closing Hours: Check-in at 3 PM, Check-out at 10 AM

3. Windchime Villa

Address: St. John, USVI (specific location provided upon booking)

Phone: (800) 562-1901

 Windchime Villa offers panoramic views of the eastern part of St. John, including Ram Head. The villa is perched high on the mountains and is designed to capture the cool Caribbean breezes. It has multiple outdoor living spaces, a fully equipped kitchen, and beautifully decorated interiors. The villa is perfect for those who want to enjoy a peaceful and secluded stay.

Unique Feature: Breathtaking views from multiple outdoor living areas.

Price Range: $4970 - $8025 per week

Opening/Closing Hours: Check-in at 3 PM, Check-out at 10 AM

4. **Waterfall Villa**

Address: Estate Enighed, St. John, USVI

Phone: (340) 776-2739

Waterfall Villa is an exquisite luxury villa located minutes from Cruz Bay. The villa features a large swimming pool, spacious suites with California king beds, and private balconies offering stunning views. The property is gated, providing extra privacy and security, making it an ideal choice for families or couples looking for a luxurious retreat.

Unique Feature: A large 35-foot swimming pool with a sunset view over the nearby islands.

Price Range: $600 - $1,200 per night

Opening/Closing Hours: Check-in at 3 PM, Check-out at 10 AM

These villas offer a variety of features and price ranges, catering to different preferences and budgets

St john usvi

while ensuring a memorable stay on the beautiful island of St. John.

Chapter 4. Cuisine and Dining
Must-Try Dishes and Drinks

The culinary landscape of St. John is a vibrant mosaic of flavors, where each bite tells a story of the island's rich cultural heritage and its connection to the land and sea. Eating here isn't just about satisfying hunger—it's about experiencing the essence of the Caribbean, savoring the warmth of the sun, the freshness of the sea, and the spice of life that defines this island paradise. As you explore the local cuisine, you'll discover that every meal is a celebration, every dish a memory in the making.

Johnnycakes

Start your culinary journey with a taste of one of St. John's most beloved comfort foods: the Johnnycake. This simple, yet deeply satisfying, fried bread is a staple on the island, enjoyed at any time of day. Whether served alongside a hearty breakfast or as a snack on its own, Johnnycakes are the kind of food that instantly makes you feel at home. Their golden, crispy exterior and soft, fluffy interior are a perfect introduction to the island's warm hospitality.

Conch Fritters

A true taste of the Caribbean, conch fritters are a must-try for any visitor to St. John. Made from fresh conch meat, finely chopped and mixed with a blend of spices and herbs, these savory fritters are deep-fried to golden perfection. Each bite is a burst of flavor, with the tender conch meat balanced by the crunch of the outer coating. Dip them in a tangy sauce, close your eyes, and let the flavors transport you to the heart of the sea.

Fish Tacos

St. John's fish tacos are more than just a meal—they're a taste of the ocean, wrapped in a warm tortilla. Freshly caught fish, often mahi-mahi or snapper, is grilled or fried and served with a vibrant mix of slaw, pico de gallo, and a drizzle of creamy sauce. The combination of textures and flavors—crisp, tender, tangy, and smooth—makes every bite a delight. Enjoy them with a view of the sea, and you'll understand why these tacos are a local favorite.

Roti

Roti, a dish that reflects the island's rich cultural tapestry, is a Caribbean take on the classic Indian flatbread wrap. Filled with curried meats, vegetables, or seafood, roti is a hearty, flavorful meal that's perfect for lunch or dinner. The tender, spiced filling wrapped in soft, flaky bread offers a satisfying taste of the island's diverse culinary influences. It's the kind of food that warms you from the inside out, whether you're enjoying it on a sunny beach or under the stars.

Callaloo

For a taste of St. John's traditional cuisine, try a bowl of callaloo, a nourishing soup made from leafy greens, often including taro or spinach, simmered with okra, onions, garlic, and a variety of spices. Sometimes enriched with meat or seafood, callaloo is a dish that brings together the earthy flavors of the land and the vibrant spices of the Caribbean. It's a soulful dish, one that connects you to the island's history and the people who have called it home for generations.

Pate

Another must-try is the island's version of the hand-held pie known as pate. These fried pastries are filled with spiced meats, seafood, or vegetables, offering a portable and delicious way to enjoy the flavors of St. John. Whether you're grabbing one from a roadside stand or enjoying it at a local eatery, a pate is the perfect snack to fuel your island explorations.

Fresh-Caught Seafood

St. John's location in the heart of the Caribbean means that fresh seafood is always on the menu. From grilled lobster to pan-seared snapper, the island's seafood dishes are as fresh as they come. Enjoying a meal of freshly caught fish, seasoned and cooked to perfection, is one of the true pleasures of island life. Pair it with a side of rice and peas, plantains, or a crisp salad, and you've got a meal that captures the essence of the sea and the spirit of the island.

Bush Tea

After a day of exploring, there's nothing quite like winding down with a cup of bush tea, a traditional herbal tea made from local plants like lemongrass, basil, or mint. Each sip is a soothing reminder of the island's natural abundance and the simple pleasures that life here offers. Whether enjoyed hot or iced, bush tea is a calming ritual that connects you to the rhythms of the island.

St John usvi

Painkiller Cocktail

No visit to St. John is complete without sipping on a Painkiller, the island's signature cocktail. A creamy blend of rum, pineapple juice, orange juice, and coconut cream, topped with a sprinkle of nutmeg, the Painkiller is the perfect drink to enjoy as the sun sets over the Caribbean. With its sweet, tropical flavors and a kick of rum, this drink embodies the laid-back, joyful spirit of the island. It's a taste of paradise in a glass, a moment of pure relaxation that you'll want to savor again and again.

Ting and Rum

For a refreshing, simple island drink, try a Ting and rum. Ting, a grapefruit-flavored soda with a tangy, citrusy punch, is a Caribbean favorite, and when mixed with local rum, it creates a drink that's both invigorating and delicious. It's the perfect beverage for a hot day, offering a cool, fizzy break from the sun, and a taste that's unmistakably Caribbean.

St john usvi

As you journey through the flavors of St. John, you'll find that each dish, each drink, is more than just a taste—it's a story, a tradition, a moment of connection with the island and its people. Whether you're savoring a fresh seafood dinner, grabbing a quick bite of local street food, or toasting the sunset with a Painkiller, the food and drink of St. John will leave an imprint on your heart, as sweet and lasting as the island itself.

Top restaurants and eateries

Here's an updated list of top restaurants and eateries in St. John, USVI, including detailed addresses, phone numbers, descriptions, unique features, price ranges, and opening hours.

1. Morgan's Mango

Address: 3-A, North Shore Rd, Cruz Bay, St. John, USVI

Phone: +1 340-693-8141

St john usvi

 A long-standing favorite, Morgan's Mango offers a Caribbean-inspired menu with Latin twists, including seafood dishes like Haitian voodoo snapper and Barbados flying fish. The restaurant is known for its vibrant atmosphere and signature cocktails.

Unique Feature: Special lobster nights on Tuesdays and Saturdays.

Price Range: Pricey

Opening Hours: Daily, 5:30 PM – 9:00 PM

2. Rhumb Lines

Address: Meada's Plaza, Cruz Bay, St. John, USVI

Phone: +1 340-776-0303

 Rhumb Lines combines Caribbean and Pacific Rim cuisine, offering dishes such as tempura shrimp and mahi-mahi in an intimate tropical garden setting. The ambiance is enhanced by bamboo torches and exotic cocktails.

St john usvi

Unique Feature: Intimate courtyard dining experience.

Price Range: Moderate

Opening Hours: Daily, 5:30 PM – 9:00 PM

3. Skinny Legs Bar & Grill

Address: 9901 Estate Emmaus, Coral Bay, St. John, USVI

Phone: +1 340-779-4982

 A laid-back, open-air bar and grill in Coral Bay, Skinny Legs is famous for its juicy burgers and relaxed atmosphere. It's a local favorite, offering comfort food without breaking the bank.

Unique Feature: No deep fryer—burgers are served with chips instead of fries.

Price Range: Affordable

Opening Hours: Daily, 11:00 AM – 9:00 PM

4. Cruz Bay Landing

Address: 6D Cruz Bay Town, St. John, USVI

Phone: +1 340-776-6908

 Located right by the ferry dock, Cruz Bay Landing serves breakfast, lunch, and dinner with a variety of Caribbean-inspired dishes. The restaurant is known for its lively atmosphere with live music every night.

Unique Feature: Extensive breakfast menu and live music every evening.

Price Range: Moderate

Opening Hours: Daily, 7:00 AM – 9:00 PM

5. The Beach Bar

Address: Wharfside Village, Cruz Bay, St. John, USVI

Phone: +1 340-777-4220

A popular spot on the beach, this bar offers a casual dining experience with a menu featuring fried seafood, tacos, and burgers. It's an ideal place for a relaxed meal with ocean views and an extensive happy hour.

Unique Feature: Long happy hours with live island music.

Price Range: Affordable

Opening Hours: Daily, 7:00 AM – 11:00 PM

These selections represent some of the best dining experiences you can enjoy in St. John, offering a mix of local flavors, unique settings, and a vibrant island atmosphere. Whether you're looking for fine dining or a casual beachside meal, these establishments provide a taste of what St. John has to offer.

Chapter 5. Must-See Attractions

Virgin Islands National Park

Virgin Islands National Park is the beating heart of St. John—a place where nature's beauty, history's echoes, and the spirit of adventure intertwine. Covering more than 60% of the island, this breathtaking park is a sanctuary for both the land and the soul, offering visitors an immersive experience in one of the most pristine natural environments in the Caribbean. As you step into the park, you're not just entering a protected area—you're stepping into a world where every trail,

St john usvi

every beach, every hidden cove tells a story of resilience, wonder, and the timeless beauty of the natural world.

Address and Location:

Virgin Islands National Park

1300 Cruz Bay Creek

St. John, U.S. Virgin Islands 00830

GPS Coordinates: 18.3422° N, 64.7387° W

A Paradise of Natural Wonders

 The park's 7,000 acres of lush forests, pristine beaches, and vibrant coral reefs offer a haven for both wildlife and those who seek to connect with the wild. Here, the air is thick with the scent of tropical flowers, the sound of rustling palms, and the distant call of birds echoing through the trees. It's a place where you can lose yourself in the rhythm of nature, where the stresses of the outside world melt away, replaced by the simple joy of being in one of the most beautiful places on Earth.

Beaches Like No Other

The park is home to some of the most stunning beaches in the Caribbean, each offering its own unique experience. Trunk Bay, with its powdery white sand and crystal-clear waters, is often hailed as one of the most beautiful beaches in the world. Its underwater snorkeling trail, complete with interpretive plaques, invites you to dive beneath the surface and explore the vibrant coral reefs teeming with colorful marine life. The experience of swimming through schools of tropical fish, with the sun filtering down through the water, is one that stays with you long after you've left the island.

Cinnamon Bay, another gem within the park, offers a quieter, more secluded experience. Here, the long stretch of sand is perfect for a peaceful day of sunbathing, swimming, or simply watching the waves roll in. The bay's calm waters make it an ideal spot for kayaking and paddleboarding, allowing you to glide across the surface and take in the stunning coastal scenery from a different perspective.

For those seeking solitude, Maho Bay and Francis Bay offer serene, less crowded beaches where you can truly connect with the natural beauty of St. John. These bays are also excellent for snorkeling, with seagrass beds just offshore that attract sea turtles and rays. The simple joy of spotting a turtle gliding gracefully through the water, its silhouette outlined against the sunlit surface, is a memory that you'll carry with you forever.

Hiking Through History

The park's network of trails offers an opportunity to explore the island's diverse landscapes, from the dry forests of the interior to the lush mangroves along the coast. The Reef Bay Trail is one of the most popular, leading you through a rich tapestry of history and nature. As you descend through the forest, you'll encounter the ruins of ancient sugar plantations, a reminder of the island's complex past. The trail also passes by petroglyphs left by the island's pre-Columbian inhabitants, their intricate carvings a silent testament to the island's deep-rooted history.

At the end of the trail, you'll be rewarded with the sight of the stunning Reef Bay, where you can cool off in the refreshing waters and soak in the tranquility of this secluded spot. Guided hikes are available, offering deeper insights into the history and ecology of the area, and providing an opportunity to learn more about the flora and fauna that make this park so special.

For a shorter, yet equally rewarding hike, the Cinnamon Bay Nature Loop offers a gentle walk through the forest, with interpretive signs that highlight the unique plants and animals of the area. This trail is perfect for families and those looking for a more leisurely experience, with the added bonus of ending near the beautiful Cinnamon Bay Beach.

Underwater Adventures

Beneath the waves, Virgin Islands National Park protects over 5,000 acres of marine environments, including coral reefs, seagrass beds, and mangroves. The park's waters are a haven for snorkelers and divers, offering some of the best underwater experiences in the Caribbean. The coral reefs are home to an astonishing variety of marine life, from colorful parrotfish and angelfish to graceful sea turtles and rays. The reefs themselves are a living tapestry of colors and shapes, with coral formations that have been growing for centuries.

For those who want to explore the underwater world, there are several snorkeling spots within the park that are easily accessible from the shore. In addition to Trunk Bay's underwater trail, Leinster Bay and Waterlemon Cay offer excellent snorkeling opportunities, with vibrant coral reefs just a short swim from the beach. Guided snorkeling tours are available, providing expert knowledge on the marine life and ecosystems that make these waters so special.

Preserving the Past

Virgin Islands National Park is not just a place of natural beauty—it's also a place of deep historical significance. The island's history is etched into the landscape, from the ruins of sugar plantations that tell the story of the island's colonial past to the petroglyphs that offer a glimpse into the lives of its earliest inhabitants. The park is dedicated to preserving these cultural treasures, ensuring that future generations can learn from and connect with the island's history.

The Annaberg Sugar Plantation, one of the most well-preserved plantation ruins on the island, offers a window into the lives of the people who lived and worked here during the 18th and 19th centuries. As you walk among the stone ruins, with the wind whispering through the trees and the sea visible in the distance, it's easy to feel the weight of history and the resilience of the people who once called this place home.

A Sanctuary for Wildlife

The park's diverse habitats support a wide range of wildlife, from the small, colorful birds that flit through the trees to the larger animals like deer and mongoose that roam the forests. Birdwatchers will find plenty to enjoy here, with species like the bananaquit, the green-throated carib, and the Caribbean dove making their home in the park. The park is also a sanctuary for endangered species, including the hawksbill turtle, which nests on the island's beaches.

As you explore the park, keep an eye out for the island's native plants, many of which have adapted to the unique conditions of this tropical paradise. The sight of a flamboyant tree in full bloom, its bright red flowers standing out against the green backdrop of the forest, is one of the many natural wonders that make this park so special.

Visitor Information and Amenities

The park's visitor center, located in Cruz Bay, is the perfect starting point for your adventure. Here, you can pick up maps, learn about the park's history and ecosystems, and get information on guided tours and activities. The rangers at the visitor center are knowledgeable and passionate about the park, and they're always happy to help you plan your visit.

Throughout the park, you'll find picnic areas, restrooms, and other amenities that make it easy to enjoy a full day of exploration. Whether you're spending the day hiking through the forest, lounging on a beach, or snorkeling in the clear waters, Virgin Islands National Park has everything you need for an unforgettable experience.

A Place to Lose—and Find—Yourself

Virgin Islands National Park is more than just a destination—it's a place where you can lose yourself in the beauty of nature and find a deeper connection with the world around you. Whether you're standing on a beach with the waves gently lapping at your feet, hiking through the forest with the sound of birdsong in your ears, or exploring the vibrant underwater world, you'll find that this park has a way of touching your soul.

As you leave the park at the end of the day, with the sun setting over the Caribbean and the memories of your visit still fresh in your mind, you'll carry with you a piece of St. John's spirit—a sense of peace, wonder, and a deeper appreciation for the natural world. Virgin Islands National Park is a place that stays with you long after you've left, a place that calls you back again and again to rediscover its magic.

Trunk Bay and the Underwater Snorkel Trail

Address and Location:

Trunk Bay, Virgin Islands National Park

St. John, U.S. Virgin Islands 00830

GPS Coordinates: 18.3494° N, 64.7695° W

 Trunk Bay is the crown jewel of St. John, a beach so breathtaking that it feels like stepping into a postcard. With its powdery white sand, crystal-clear turquoise waters, and lush green backdrop, Trunk Bay is the epitome of paradise. This iconic spot, often ranked among the world's most beautiful beaches, invites visitors to bask in its natural splendor, where every moment feels like a dream come true.

The Underwater Snorkel Trail

But Trunk Bay's beauty isn't just confined to its shores. Just a short swim from the beach lies the famous Underwater Snorkel Trail, a unique attraction that adds an element of adventure to your visit. The trail, marked by underwater signs, guides snorkelers through vibrant coral reefs teeming with marine life. As you glide through the warm, clear waters, you'll encounter schools of colorful fish, playful rays, and perhaps even a graceful sea turtle.

This underwater journey offers more than just a visual feast—it's an opportunity to connect with the ocean in a profound way. The gentle sway of the currents, the kaleidoscope of colors, and the silence of the underwater world create a meditative experience that lingers long after you've left the water.

A Place of Serenity and Wonder

Whether you're snorkeling along the trail, lounging on the sand, or simply gazing out at the horizon, Trunk Bay is a place where time seems to stand still. It's a sanctuary of serenity and wonder, a place where the beauty of nature washes over you, leaving you with a sense of peace and fulfillment. As you leave Trunk Bay, the memories of its stunning vistas and vibrant underwater world will stay with you, a reminder of the magic that St. John holds.

Annaberg Plantation Ruins

Address and Location:

Annaberg Plantation Ruins, Virgin Islands National Park

St john usvi

St. John, U.S. Virgin Islands 00830

GPS Coordinates: 18.3610° N, 64.7253° W

 The Annaberg Plantation Ruins are not just remnants of old stone buildings—they are echoes of a past that shaped the very soul of St. John. Tucked away in the verdant hills of the island, overlooking the azure waters of the Caribbean Sea, these ruins stand as a poignant reminder of the island's history, a history marked by both hardship and resilience. As you walk through the ruins, you can almost hear the whispers of the past, feel the weight of history in the air, and connect with the stories of the people who once lived and worked here.

A Journey Through Time

Annaberg was once one of the largest sugar plantations on St. John, a bustling estate where sugar, molasses, and rum were produced in the 18th and 19th centuries. The ruins that remain today—the windmill, the sugar factory, the slave quarters—are hauntingly beautiful, their weathered stones and moss-covered walls telling a story of an era long gone but never forgotten. As you explore the site, it's easy to imagine the plantation in its heyday, with the windmill's blades turning in the breeze, the smell of molasses thick in the air, and the sounds of labor echoing through the fields.

The walk through Annaberg is a journey through time, one that brings you face to face with the island's colonial past and the realities of life on a sugar plantation. The ruins are a testament to the endurance of the enslaved Africans who were forced to work here, their strength and resilience woven into the fabric of St. John's history. Standing in the shadow of the windmill, with the Caribbean Sea stretching out before you, it's impossible not to feel the gravity of what took place here, and the deep connection between the island's past and its present.

Cultural and Historical Significance

The significance of Annaberg goes beyond its physical remnants. It is a place where the cultural heritage of St. John comes alive, a place where the stories of the enslaved people who lived here are honored and remembered. The park offers interpretive displays and guided tours that provide insight into the daily lives of those who worked on the plantation, as well as the broader history of the sugar industry in the Caribbean.

One of the most moving experiences at Annaberg is the opportunity to learn about the traditions and skills that were passed down through generations. From basket weaving to bread making, these cultural practices are a testament to the resilience and ingenuity of the people who endured the hardships of plantation life. The ruins, in their quiet dignity, stand as a tribute to their legacy, reminding visitors of the strength of the human spirit.

A View Like No Other

Beyond its historical significance, Annaberg offers one of the most breathtaking views on the island. From the top of the hill, where the windmill stands sentinel, you can gaze out over the sparkling waters of the Caribbean, with the British Virgin Islands visible in the distance. It's a view that takes your breath away, one that captures the beauty and tranquility of St. John in a single, sweeping panorama. As you stand there, with the wind rustling through the trees and the sun casting a golden glow over the ruins, it's easy to understand why this place is so special.

A Place of Reflection

Visiting the Annaberg Plantation Ruins is more than just a historical tour—it's a deeply emotional experience. It's a place where you can reflect on the complexities of history, the enduring strength of the human spirit, and the ways in which the past continues to shape the present. Whether you're a history enthusiast, a nature lover, or simply someone seeking a

St john usvi

deeper connection with the island, Annaberg offers a unique and powerful experience.

As you leave the ruins and make your way back down the hill, you'll carry with you a piece of St. John's history—a history that is as much about the struggles of the past as it is about the hope and resilience that continue to define the island today. The Annaberg Plantation Ruins are a place where history comes alive, a place where the stories of the past are honored, and a place where the beauty of St. John shines through in every stone, every breeze, and every view.

Cinnamon Bay and Water Sports

Address and Location:

Cinnamon Bay, Virgin Islands National Park

St. John, U.S. Virgin Islands 00830

GPS Coordinates: 18.3522° N, 64.7643° W

Cinnamon Bay is a place where the beauty of St. John truly shines—a long, wide stretch of powdery white sand, framed by lush, green hills and kissed by the gentle waves of the Caribbean Sea. It's a place where time slows down, where the worries of the world melt away, and where the natural beauty of the island takes center stage. Whether you're looking to relax on the beach, explore the underwater world, or embark on a water adventure, Cinnamon Bay offers something for everyone.

A Beach That Beckons

The first thing you notice as you arrive at Cinnamon Bay is the sheer expanse of the beach. It's one of the largest beaches on St. John, with plenty of space to spread out and find your own little slice of paradise. The sand here is soft and inviting, perfect for lounging under the sun, building sandcastles with the kids, or taking a leisurely stroll along the shore. The water is a stunning shade of turquoise, so clear that you can see the sand beneath your feet as you wade in. The gentle waves make it ideal for swimming, and the calm, shallow waters near the shore are perfect for young children.

As you sit on the beach, with the warm sun on your face and the sound of the waves in your ears, it's easy to lose yourself in the beauty of the moment. The backdrop of the surrounding hills, dotted with swaying palms and vibrant tropical plants, adds to the sense of tranquility. Cinnamon Bay is a place where you can simply be—where you can take a deep breath, close your eyes, and feel the stress of everyday life fade away.

A Haven for Water Sports Enthusiasts

For those who crave a bit more adventure, Cinnamon Bay is a water sports paradise. The calm waters and consistent breezes make it an ideal spot for a variety of activities, whether you're an experienced water sports enthusiast or trying something new for the first time.

Snorkeling:

Just off the shore, the underwater world of Cinnamon Bay beckons. Grab your snorkel gear and dive into the clear waters to discover a vibrant coral reef teeming with marine life. The reef is home to a dazzling array of fish, from bright parrotfish to elusive barracudas, and if you're lucky, you might even spot a sea turtle gliding gracefully through the water. The bay's protected status within Virgin Islands National Park ensures that the marine environment is pristine, offering some of the best snorkeling on the island. Every snorkel session is a new adventure, a chance to connect with the ocean and witness the beauty of the reef up close.

Kayaking and Paddleboarding:

Cinnamon Bay's calm waters are perfect for kayaking and paddleboarding, allowing you to explore the bay and the nearby coastline at your own pace. Renting a kayak or paddleboard is easy, and once you're out on the water, you'll be treated to stunning views of the beach and the surrounding hills. Paddling along the coast, you can explore hidden coves, spot sea birds, and enjoy the peaceful rhythm of being on the water. It's an experience that brings you closer to nature, a chance to see the island from a different perspective and appreciate its beauty in a whole new way.

Sailing and Windsurfing:

For those who love to sail, Cinnamon Bay offers excellent conditions for windsurfing and small sailboats. The steady trade winds provide just the right amount of breeze to catch your sail and glide across the water. Sailing in Cinnamon Bay is an exhilarating experience, with the wind in your hair, the sun on your face, and the vast expanse of the Caribbean stretching out before you. Windsurfing lessons are available for beginners, and experienced sailors can rent equipment and head out to explore the bay. It's a thrill that's hard to match, a perfect combination of skill and the natural elements.

Cultural and Historical Significance

Beyond its natural beauty and recreational opportunities, Cinnamon Bay is also a place of cultural and historical significance. The nearby Cinnamon Bay Plantation ruins offer a glimpse into the island's past, with remnants of the old sugar plantation that once thrived here. A short hike from the beach will take you to these fascinating ruins, where you can learn about the history of the plantation and the people who lived and worked here. The site is a reminder of St. John's rich and complex history, adding a layer of depth to your visit.

A Place to Connect with Nature

Cinnamon Bay is not just a destination—it's an experience, a place where you can connect with the natural world and find a sense of peace and joy that's hard to come by in the hustle and bustle of everyday life. Whether you're spending the day swimming, snorkeling, kayaking, or simply lounging on the beach, Cinnamon Bay offers a perfect blend of relaxation and adventure.

As the day draws to a close and the sun begins to set, casting a warm, golden light over the bay, you'll find yourself lingering on the beach, reluctant to leave. The beauty of Cinnamon Bay stays with you, a memory of a perfect day in paradise, a reminder of the simple, yet profound, joy of being in nature. It's a place that calls you back, again and again, to experience its magic and lose yourself in its endless charm.

Chapter 6. Activities and Adventures

Snorkeling and Diving Hotspots

Address and Location:

Various locations around St. John, U.S. Virgin Islands

Key Spots Include:

- Trunk Bay: Virgin Islands National Park, St. John, USVI 00830

- Waterlemon Cay: Leinster Bay, St. John, USVI 00830

- Hansen Bay: East End, St. John, USVI 00830

- Salt Pond Bay: Coral Bay, St. John, USVI 00830

St. John's underwater world is a vibrant tapestry of life, color, and wonder—a hidden paradise waiting to be discovered by those who dare to explore beneath the waves. From the novice snorkeler to the seasoned

93

diver, the island's waters offer an array of experiences that are nothing short of magical. The reefs here are alive with marine life, the water is warm and inviting, and every dive or snorkel is an adventure that lingers long after you've returned to shore.

Trunk Bay: The Iconic Underwater Trail

Trunk Bay, one of the island's most famous beaches, is also home to the iconic Underwater Snorkel Trail. This self-guided trail, marked by underwater plaques, leads you through a coral garden where you'll encounter a dazzling array of sea life. From the brightly colored parrotfish to the graceful stingrays that glide along the sandy bottom, every turn of the head reveals something new and breathtaking. The clear, shallow waters make it ideal for beginners, while the abundance of marine life keeps even the most experienced snorkelers captivated. The beauty of Trunk Bay extends beyond its shores, inviting you to dive into an underwater world that's as stunning as the landscape above.

Waterlemon Cay: A Snorkeler's Dream

Tucked away in Leinster Bay, Waterlemon Cay is a snorkeler's dream. The small cay, surrounded by crystal-clear waters, is known for its rich marine life and vibrant coral formations. The short swim from the shore to the cay is well worth the effort, as you're greeted by a reef teeming with life. Schools of tropical fish dart in and out of the corals, while starfish and sea cucumbers decorate the sandy bottom. The waters around Waterlemon Cay are also frequented by sea turtles, who can often be seen grazing on the seagrass or surfacing for air. Snorkeling here is a serene, almost meditative experience, where the beauty of the underwater world unfolds slowly, revealing its secrets to those who take the time to look.

Hansen Bay: The Hidden Gem

On the quieter East End of St. John lies Hansen Bay, a hidden gem known for its excellent snorkeling and tranquil waters. The bay's calm, protected waters make it perfect for a leisurely snorkel, allowing you to explore at your own pace. The coral reef here is healthy and vibrant, home to a wide variety of fish, including angelfish, butterflyfish, and even the occasional octopus. The seagrass beds in the shallows are a haven for turtles, who can often be spotted feeding or resting on the ocean floor. Hansen Bay is less crowded than some of the island's more popular spots, offering a more intimate and peaceful snorkeling experience. It's a place where you can truly connect with nature, surrounded by the beauty and stillness of the underwater world.

Salt Pond Bay: The Diver's Paradise

For those looking to venture deeper, Salt Pond Bay on the island's southeastern coast offers some of the best diving on St. John. The bay's outer reef drops off into deeper waters, creating a stunning underwater landscape of coral cliffs, sea fans, and sponges. The diverse topography attracts a variety of marine life, from schools of snapper and jacks to the occasional reef shark. The bay is also home to several underwater caves and tunnels, which are thrilling to explore for more experienced divers. Salt Pond Bay's relative seclusion and unspoiled beauty make it a favorite among divers seeking adventure and discovery. Whether you're exploring the vibrant reef or descending into the depths, diving at Salt Pond Bay is an experience that stays with you, a journey into a world that's as mysterious as it is beautiful.

A Journey into the Blue

Snorkeling and diving in St. John is more than just a recreational activity—it's a journey into the heart of the island's natural beauty, a chance to connect with the ocean in a way that's both thrilling and humbling. The waters around St. John are alive with color and movement, a dynamic ecosystem where every dive or snorkel offers something new to discover.

Whether you're drifting over a coral garden, swimming alongside a sea turtle, or exploring the depths of an underwater cave, each moment spent in the water is a reminder of the incredible diversity and beauty of the marine world. The island's snorkeling and diving hotspots are more than just destinations— they are gateways to another world, where the magic of the ocean comes alive in every ripple, every ray of light, and every creature that crosses your path.

As you emerge from the water, the sun warming your skin and the salt lingering on your lips, you'll carry with you the memories of your underwater adventures—a kaleidoscope of colors, the thrill of discovery, and the deep sense of peace that comes from being immersed in nature. Snorkeling and diving in St. John is an experience that stays with you long after you've left the island, a connection to the ocean that calls you back, again and again, to explore its depths and uncover its mysteries.

Hiking Trails and Nature Walks

Key Trails Include:

- Reef Bay Trail: Virgin Islands National Park, St. John, USVI 00830

- Ram Head Trail: Salt Pond Bay, St. John, USVI 00830

- Lind Point Trail: Cruz Bay, St. John, USVI 00830

- Cinnamon Bay Trail: Cinnamon Bay, St. John, USVI 00830

St. John is more than just a beach lover's paradise; it's a hiker's haven, where every trail invites you to step off the beaten path and into the island's untamed beauty. The hiking trails of St. John are gateways to adventure, winding through lush tropical forests, along rugged coastlines, and up to panoramic vistas that take your breath away. Each step on these trails is a journey into the heart of the island, where nature's wonders reveal themselves in the rustle of leaves, the song of birds, and the scent of the ocean breeze.

Reef Bay Trail: A Journey Through Time and Nature

The Reef Bay Trail is a must-do for any hiker visiting St. John, offering a rich blend of natural beauty and historical intrigue. The trailhead begins near Centerline Road and descends through dense tropical forest, where the sounds of the jungle envelop you—chirping birds, rustling leaves, and the occasional rustle of a lizard darting across your path. As you make your way down the trail, you'll encounter ancient petroglyphs, carved into the rock by the island's indigenous Taino people. These mysterious symbols are a reminder of the deep connection between the island's history and its natural landscape.

The trail continues past the ruins of the Reef Bay Sugar Mill, where you can explore the remnants of St. John's colonial past, including the old sugar factory and the towering stone chimney. The journey culminates at the serene Reef Bay Beach, where the jungle meets the sea in a quiet, secluded cove. Here, you can rest and take in the beauty of the Caribbean before making the return trek. The Reef Bay Trail is more than just a hike—it's a journey through time, a chance to connect with the island's rich history and vibrant natural world.

Ram Head Trail: The Ultimate Coastal Adventure

For those seeking dramatic coastal views and a challenging hike, the Ram Head Trail is an unforgettable experience. Starting at Salt Pond Bay, the trail takes you along a rugged coastline, with the turquoise waters of the Caribbean on one side and the arid, cactus-studded landscape on the other. The path is rocky and exposed, but the rewards are worth every step. As you climb higher, the views become more and more breathtaking, with the vast expanse of the ocean stretching out before you and the distant silhouette of St. Croix on the horizon.

The trail ends at the very tip of Ram Head, where you'll stand atop a windswept bluff, surrounded by nothing but sky and sea. The feeling of being at the edge of the world, with the waves crashing against the rocks far below, is exhilarating. It's a place where you can feel the power of nature, where the wind carries the scent of salt and the sun bathes everything in a golden glow. The Ram Head Trail is a hike for the adventurous, a journey that challenges the body and rewards the spirit with views that linger long after you've returned to the trailhead.

Lind Point Trail: A Gateway to St. John's Natural Beauty

The Lind Point Trail is perfect for those looking for an accessible yet rewarding hike close to Cruz Bay. This popular trail begins near the Virgin Islands National Park Visitor Center and winds its way through dry forest, offering occasional glimpses of the sparkling blue waters below. The trail splits into two paths: the upper trail, which climbs gently to the Lind Point overlook, and the lower trail, which takes you directly to Honeymoon Beach. The overlook offers a stunning panoramic view of Cruz Bay, the surrounding cays, and even St. Thomas in the distance—a perfect spot to pause and take in the beauty of the island.

The trail is easy to moderate, making it a great choice for families or those new to hiking. The reward at the end of the hike is Honeymoon Beach, one of the island's most beautiful and serene beaches. Here, you can cool off in the clear waters, relax on the soft sand, or continue exploring by renting a kayak or paddleboard. The Lind Point Trail is more than just a hike—it's a gateway to some of St. John's most stunning natural beauty, a reminder that adventure is never far from wherever you are on the island.

Cinnamon Bay Trail: A Hike Through History

The Cinnamon Bay Trail offers a short but steep hike through lush forest, leading to the historic ruins of the Cinnamon Bay Plantation. The trailhead is located near Cinnamon Bay Beach, and the path winds upward through a dense canopy of trees, where the air is thick with the scent of tropical flowers and the calls of native birds echo through the forest. Along the way, you'll pass by towering kapok trees, their massive roots stretching across the trail, and the remains of ancient stone walls, overgrown with vines and moss.

At the end of the trail, you'll find the ruins of the plantation's great house and sugar factory, a stark reminder of the island's colonial past. The view from here is stunning, with the green hills of St. John stretching out before you and the blue waters of Cinnamon Bay glistening in the distance. The Cinnamon Bay Trail is a hike that combines natural beauty with historical intrigue, offering a glimpse into the island's past while immersing you in its lush, tropical landscape.

Whether you're trekking through dense forest, following a rocky coastline, or exploring the ruins of a bygone era, hiking on St. John is an adventure that stays with you. It's a journey of discovery, not just of the island's landscapes, but of your own connection to the natural world. The trails of St. John are waiting, ready to lead you on an unforgettable adventure into the heart of paradise.

Boating, Sailing, and Kayaking

The allure of St. John extends far beyond its shores. The waters surrounding this island paradise beckon with promises of adventure, tranquility, and discovery. Whether you're sailing into the horizon, kayaking through hidden coves, or simply drifting along the gentle waves, the experience of being on the water in St. John is nothing short of magical. It's a chance to see the island from a new perspective, to explore the unknown, and to connect with the beauty and serenity that the sea offers.

Sailing: Embracing the Wind and Waves

There's a timeless romance to sailing—hoisting the sails, feeling the wind catch, and gliding across the open water with nothing but the sound of the waves and the call of seabirds in your ears. In St. John, sailing isn't just an activity; it's an invitation to adventure. The trade winds that blow through the Virgin Islands create perfect conditions for sailing, whether you're a seasoned sailor or a curious beginner.

Set out from Cruz Bay or Coral Bay, and soon you'll find yourself leaving the bustling shores behind, heading towards the endless blue of the Caribbean. As the island recedes into the distance, you'll discover a sense of freedom that only the open water can provide. You can chart your own course, exploring the nearby cays and islets, each with its own unique charm. Anchor at a secluded bay, where the water is so clear you can see the fish swimming below, or sail towards the horizon, where the sky meets the sea in a breathtaking panorama.

For those looking to deepen their sailing experience, many operators offer day trips or multi-day charters, complete with a knowledgeable crew who can guide you through the islands, sharing their favorite hidden spots and local stories. Whether you're seeking adventure, relaxation, or a bit of both, sailing in St. John is an unforgettable way to experience the island's beauty.

Boating: Exploring the Hidden Gems

Boating around St. John opens up a world of possibilities. The island is surrounded by an array of smaller cays and reefs, each one offering something special—whether it's a pristine beach, a prime snorkeling spot, or a secluded hideaway where you can escape the world. Renting a powerboat or joining a guided boat tour allows you to explore these hidden gems at your own pace.

Imagine cruising along the coastline, the wind in your hair, the sun on your face, as you make your way to a deserted beach where the only footprints in the sand are your own. Or perhaps you'll stop at one of the many snorkeling spots, where the underwater world is alive with color and life, waiting to be discovered. For a true Caribbean experience, visit one of the floating bars in the area—like the famous Lime Out on nearby Hansen Bay—where you can enjoy a refreshing drink while lounging in the turquoise waters.

The beauty of boating in St. John lies in its flexibility. You can spend the day exploring, hopping from one pristine location to the next, or simply drop anchor and let the world drift by. Whether you're with family, friends, or on a romantic escape, the experience of boating around St. John is one that will stay with you, a memory of sun-soaked days and endless blue horizons.

St john usvi

Kayaking: A Journey into Serenity

For those who prefer to experience the water at a slower pace, kayaking offers a serene and intimate way to explore the island's coastline. With each stroke of the paddle, you'll glide through calm, crystal-clear waters, hugging the shoreline and discovering the island's hidden treasures up close.

Kayaking in St. John is a chance to connect with nature in a deeply personal way. You can paddle through the mangrove forests of Hurricane Hole, where the roots of the trees reach down into the water, creating a labyrinth of tunnels to explore. Here, the water is so clear that you can see the marine life below—fish darting among the roots, crabs scuttling along the sandy bottom, and, if you're lucky, a gentle stingray gliding by.

Or perhaps you'll venture to one of the island's many quiet bays, where the only sound is the soft splash of your paddle and the distant call of a seabird. The gentle rhythm of kayaking allows you to take in the beauty of your surroundings—the vibrant greens of the hills, the sparkling blue of the water, the warmth of the sun on your skin.

For a truly unique experience, consider a guided night kayak tour, where you'll paddle under the stars, the water glowing with bioluminescence as your paddle disturbs the tiny organisms that light up the sea. It's a magical experience, one that feels like stepping into another world, where the boundaries between land, sea, and sky blur into a single, awe-inspiring moment.

The Call of the Sea

Boating, sailing, and kayaking in St. John are more than just activities—they're ways to connect with the island's soul, to experience its beauty from a perspective that few get to see. Whether you're navigating the open water, exploring a hidden cove, or simply drifting with the current, there's a sense of peace and wonder that comes from being on the sea.

The waters around St. John are a playground for those who seek adventure, a sanctuary for those who crave peace, and a canvas for those who wish to paint their own story of the island. The call of the sea is strong here, and once you've answered it, it's a sound that will stay with you long after you've left the island's shores.

Shopping and Local Markets

St. John's charm isn't just found in its beaches and forests; it also thrives in the vibrant energy of its local markets and shops. Walking through the streets of Cruz Bay or Coral Bay, you'll find a tapestry of color, creativity, and culture woven into every corner. Here, shopping isn't just about finding souvenirs—it's about connecting with the island's spirit, supporting its artisans, and bringing a piece of its magic home with you.

Cruz Bay: The Heart of Island Shopping

Cruz Bay, the island's main town, is where shopping meets storytelling. As you wander through its winding streets, you'll discover a delightful mix of boutiques, galleries, and open-air markets, each one offering something unique. The shops in Cruz Bay aren't just stores; they're expressions of the island's vibrant culture, each item telling a story of the hands that crafted it and the traditions that inspired it.

In the bustling Mongoose Junction, a shopping complex with a distinctly Caribbean flair, you'll find a curated selection of high-quality goods, from handcrafted jewelry and art to stylish resort wear and home decor. Each piece reflects the island's natural beauty—jewelry adorned with pearls and seashells, paintings that capture the turquoise waters, and textiles in vibrant tropical hues. The local artisans pour their heart into every creation, infusing each piece with a sense of place and passion.

If you're looking for something truly special, stop by the local art galleries, where you can admire and purchase works by St. John's talented artists. Whether it's a vivid painting of the island's landscapes, a sculpture carved from native wood, or a piece of jewelry inspired by the sea, these works of art are more than just souvenirs—they're pieces of St. John's soul, captured in a moment of creativity.

Coral Bay: A Bohemian Treasure Trove

On the quieter side of the island, Coral Bay offers a more laid-back, bohemian shopping experience. Here, the vibe is relaxed and unhurried, with shops that reflect the eclectic spirit of the community. You'll find a mix of local crafts, vintage finds, and one-of-a-kind treasures that speak to the free-spirited nature of this part of the island.

The small, locally-owned shops in Coral Bay are a joy to explore. Step into a boutique filled with handwoven baskets, locally-made pottery, and whimsical artwork, each item reflecting the creativity and resourcefulness of the island's artisans. You might find a hand-dyed sarong perfect for the beach, a piece of driftwood art that captures the essence of the island, or a jar of homemade jam bursting with the flavors of the tropics.

The vibe in Coral Bay is all about sustainability and supporting local makers. Many of the goods are made from recycled or locally-sourced materials, reflecting the community's commitment to preserving the island's natural beauty. As you browse through the offerings, you'll feel a deep connection to the island's way of life—a slower, more mindful approach to living that values craftsmanship, creativity, and the environment.

Local Markets: The Pulse of the Island

For a true taste of local life, there's nothing quite like visiting one of St. John's local markets. These markets are the heartbeat of the island, where locals and visitors alike gather to share in the bounty of the land

and sea. The market stalls overflow with fresh produce, handmade crafts, and delicious local treats, offering a sensory experience that's as vibrant as the island itself.

At the weekly farmer's markets, you'll find tables piled high with tropical fruits, fragrant herbs, and freshly-caught seafood. The air is filled with the scent of ripe mangoes, sweet pineapples, and spicy peppers, each one picked at the peak of freshness. The farmers and fishermen who sell their goods are happy to chat, sharing stories about the island's history, its natural rhythms, and the best ways to enjoy their offerings.

These markets are also a great place to find locally-made crafts, from woven baskets and handmade candles to intricate beadwork and colorful paintings. Each item is a labor of love, crafted with care and infused with the spirit of the island. Whether you're picking up a handmade piece of jewelry, a bottle of locally-produced rum, or a jar of hot sauce made from island-grown peppers, you're not just buying a product—you're taking home a piece of St. John's culture.

A Shopping Experience Like No Other

Shopping in St. John isn't about rushing through aisles or hunting for bargains. It's about slowing down, savoring the moment, and connecting with the people and stories behind each item. It's about supporting local artisans who pour their hearts into their work, creating pieces that are as unique as the island itself.

As you explore the shops and markets, you'll find that shopping in St. John is more than just a transaction—it's an experience. It's the warm smile of a shopkeeper, the stories shared over a handcrafted item, the joy of discovering something that speaks to you in a way no mass-produced item ever could. It's about taking a piece of St. John home with you, a reminder of the island's beauty, creativity, and spirit that will stay with you long after your trip is over.

So, whether you're looking for a unique piece of art, a handcrafted keepsake, or simply a taste of the island's flavors, shopping in St. John is an adventure in itself. It's a journey through the island's culture, its creativity, and its soul—one that leaves you with more than just souvenirs, but memories and connections that last a lifetime.

Chapter 7. Suggested Itineraries

Family-Friendly Itinerary

St. John, with its breathtaking landscapes and warm Caribbean spirit, is a place where family memories are made. The island's natural beauty, combined with its welcoming atmosphere, creates the perfect backdrop for a vacation that every member of the family will cherish. Whether you're seeking adventure, relaxation, or a mix of both, St. John offers a family-friendly itinerary that's filled with moments of wonder, joy, and connection.

Day 1: Arrival and Settling In

Your family's journey begins with the arrival on St. John, where the island's tranquil pace and stunning scenery will immediately embrace you. After settling into your accommodations, take a leisurely stroll through Cruz Bay. This charming town is the heart of the island, offering a glimpse into its laid-back lifestyle. Stop by one of the local cafés for a refreshing drink, and let the kids indulge in some island-made ice cream—rich with tropical flavors like mango, coconut, and guava.

As the sun begins to set, head to one of the island's family-friendly restaurants. Many places offer outdoor seating, where you can dine under the stars while enjoying the cool evening breeze. Try local dishes that even the youngest travelers will love—think grilled fish, fried plantains, and fresh fruit smoothies. It's a gentle start to your adventure, allowing everyone to unwind and settle into island time.

Day 2: Beach Day at Trunk Bay

No trip to St. John would be complete without a day at Trunk Bay, one of the most famous and family-friendly beaches in the Caribbean. The soft, white sand and calm, shallow waters make it a perfect spot for kids to play and explore. Pack a picnic and spend the day building sandcastles, splashing in the turquoise waters, and soaking up the sun.

Trunk Bay is also home to the famous Underwater Snorkel Trail, a must-do for families. Even if you've never snorkeled before, the clear, shallow waters make it easy and fun for everyone. Follow the trail and discover the vibrant coral reefs and colorful fish that call this bay home. The experience of exploring the underwater world together is one that your family will talk about for years to come.

After a day of sun and sea, return to Cruz Bay for dinner. Choose a casual spot where the kids can continue their beach fun with sand beneath their feet while you enjoy a delicious meal with your toes in the sand. It's the perfect way to end a day filled with simple, sun-soaked pleasures.

Day 3: Exploring Virgin Islands National Park

The third day of your family adventure takes you into the heart of St. John's natural beauty—Virgin Islands National Park. Start your day with a visit to the park's visitor center in Cruz Bay, where you can learn about the park's history, wildlife, and the many activities available. The park rangers often have educational programs for children, offering a fun and interactive way to learn about the island's ecosystems.

From there, embark on an easy hike along the Cinnamon Bay Nature Trail. This family-friendly trail winds through lush forest and historical ruins, offering a glimpse into the island's past and its natural wonders. The kids will love spotting tropical birds, lizards, and maybe even a deer or two along the way.

After your hike, head to Cinnamon Bay Beach, where the calm waters and long stretch of sand are perfect for more beach fun. Rent kayaks or paddleboards for some family-friendly water adventures, or simply relax on the shore with a good book while the kids play in the sand.

In the evening, gather the family for a barbecue at one of the park's picnic areas. Watch as the sun sets behind the hills, painting the sky in shades of pink and orange. It's a moment of pure serenity, where the only sounds are the laughter of your children and the gentle rustling of the palm trees.

Day 4: A Day of Adventure in Coral Bay

Day four takes you to the quieter side of the island— Coral Bay. Known for its bohemian vibe and stunning natural surroundings, Coral Bay offers a mix of adventure and relaxation. Start your day with a horseback riding tour through the hills of the Carolina Valley. Suitable for all ages, these guided tours offer a unique way to see the island's landscape, with

St john usvi

panoramic views of the ocean and the surrounding islands.

After your ride, explore the local shops and markets in Coral Bay. The kids will enjoy browsing through the eclectic offerings, from handmade crafts to quirky souvenirs. Stop for lunch at one of the casual eateries, where you can enjoy fresh seafood and island specialties in a relaxed, open-air setting.

In the afternoon, take a family-friendly boat tour around the island's eastern shores. Many tours offer opportunities for snorkeling, swimming, and even dolphin spotting. The boat's crew will entertain the kids with stories of pirate legends and island history, while you relax and take in the stunning views.

Return to your accommodations for a quiet evening. Order in some local fare and have a cozy family movie night, reflecting on the day's adventures and looking forward to the final day on the island.

Day 5: A Final Day of Fun and Relaxation

On your last full day on St. John, make the most of the island's offerings with a mix of relaxation and adventure. Start with a visit to Maho Bay, another family-friendly beach where the shallow waters are perfect for young children. Maho Bay is known for its sea turtles, and with a bit of luck, you'll spot these gentle creatures swimming nearby.

Spend the morning swimming, snorkeling, or simply relaxing on the beach, soaking up the last of the island's sunshine. For lunch, visit one of the nearby food trucks or beachside cafés, where you can enjoy fresh, local dishes with your toes in the sand.

In the afternoon, take a scenic drive along the North Shore Road, stopping at the overlooks to take in the breathtaking views. It's a moment to capture with photos, a reminder of the island's beauty that you'll carry with you long after you've returned home.

End your day with a farewell dinner at one of St. John's family-friendly restaurants. Choose a spot with a view, where you can watch the sun set over the water, casting a golden glow on your last evening in paradise. Share your favorite memories of the trip over a delicious meal, toasting to the adventures you've had and the memories you've made.

Day 6: Departure and Reflection

As your time on St. John comes to an end, take a moment to reflect on the experiences you've shared as a family. The island has a way of bringing people together, creating bonds that are strengthened by the beauty of the surroundings and the joy of shared adventures.

As you board the ferry back to St. Thomas, watch the island fade into the distance, carrying with you the sounds of the waves, the warmth of the sun, and the laughter of your loved ones. St. John has a way of staying with you, long after the trip is over—a place where your family created memories that will be treasured for a lifetime.

Adventure Seekers Itinerary

For those with a thirst for adrenaline and a love of the great outdoors, St. John is a playground of untamed beauty and thrilling experiences. The island's rugged terrain, vibrant marine life, and hidden treasures offer endless opportunities for adventure. Whether you're scaling the heights of its hills, diving into its crystal-clear waters, or exploring its untamed wilderness, this itinerary is designed for the adventurer at heart—those who crave the rush of discovery and the thrill of the unknown.

St john usvi

Day 1: Arrival and a Sunset Hike

Your adventure begins as soon as you set foot on St. John. After settling into your accommodations, get acquainted with the island's natural beauty with a sunset hike to Ram Head. This trail, located at the island's southeastern tip, offers an exhilarating start to your journey. As you ascend the rocky path, the landscape unfolds beneath you—rugged cliffs, sweeping ocean views, and the dramatic interplay of light and shadow as the sun dips below the horizon.

The trail's end rewards you with one of the most breathtaking panoramas on the island. The sun sets the sky ablaze with hues of orange, pink, and purple, casting a golden glow on the turquoise waters below. Standing at the edge of the cliff, with the wind in your hair and the ocean stretching out before you, you'll feel a profound sense of awe and exhilaration—a perfect introduction to the adventures that lie ahead.

Day 2: Exploring Virgin Islands National Park

The second day of your adventure takes you deep into the heart of Virgin Islands National Park, a vast expanse of wilderness that covers over 60% of the island. Start your day early with a challenging hike along the Reef Bay Trail, one of the park's most iconic routes. This trail winds through lush tropical forests, past ancient petroglyphs carved by the island's indigenous people, and down to the secluded Reef Bay Beach. The trail's descent is steep and demanding, but the reward is well worth the effort—a pristine, often deserted beach where you can cool off in the clear waters or explore the ruins of a 19th-century sugar plantation.

For the truly adventurous, continue your exploration with a guided tour of the park's hidden waterfalls. Accessible only by foot or by kayak, these waterfalls are a well-kept secret, offering a secluded oasis of natural beauty. The hike to the falls is challenging, but the sight of the water cascading down the rocky cliffs into crystal-clear pools is nothing short of magical.

St john usvi

Take a refreshing dip in the cool waters, surrounded by the sounds of the jungle and the scent of wildflowers.

In the evening, head back to Cruz Bay to refuel at one of the island's lively eateries. Enjoy a hearty meal of local seafood and island flavors, recharging your energy for the next day's adventures.

Day 3: A Day on the Water

No adventure in St. John would be complete without exploring the island's vibrant underwater world. Start your day with an early morning snorkeling trip to Waterlemon Cay, one of the island's premier snorkeling spots. The waters around the cay are teeming with marine life—colorful coral reefs, schools of tropical fish, and, if you're lucky, the occasional sea turtle or stingray. The currents here can be strong, adding an extra element of excitement as you navigate the underwater terrain.

St john usvi

After a morning of snorkeling, take your adventure to the next level with a sailing excursion around the island. Charter a sailboat and let the wind carry you across the Caribbean Sea, with stops at some of the island's most secluded beaches and hidden coves. Many charters offer the opportunity to try your hand at sailing, giving you a taste of the thrill and skill involved in navigating these waters. For those seeking an even bigger adrenaline rush, consider adding a session of windsurfing or kiteboarding to your day. The island's steady trade winds and open waters create ideal conditions for these high-octane sports.

As the day draws to a close, drop anchor in one of the island's tranquil bays and enjoy a sunset dinner on the water. The sky ablaze with color, the gentle rocking of the boat, and the sounds of the ocean create a serene yet exhilarating end to an action-packed day.

Day 4: Off-Roading and Secret Beaches

Day four is all about exploring the island's lesser-known treasures. Start with an off-road adventure through the island's rugged interior. Rent a 4x4 vehicle and set out on the island's challenging backroads, navigating steep hills, rocky paths, and dense forests. The journey will take you to some of the island's most remote and beautiful locations—hidden beaches, secluded bays, and panoramic viewpoints that few visitors ever see.

One such hidden gem is Lameshur Bay, a secluded beach on the island's southern coast. Accessible only by a rough dirt road, this beach is a haven for adventurers. The bay's clear, calm waters are perfect for snorkeling, while the surrounding hills offer opportunities for hiking and exploring. Pack a picnic and spend the day swimming, snorkeling, and soaking up the sun in this tranquil, off-the-beaten-path paradise.

For those who crave even more adventure, continue your off-roading journey to Ram Head, where you can embark on a challenging hike up the rocky cliffs for stunning views of the surrounding islands. The rugged terrain and strong winds make this hike a true test of endurance and determination, but the sense of accomplishment you'll feel at the top is unmatched.

Day 5: Kayaking and Nighttime Exploration

Your final day on St. John offers one last adventure—a day of kayaking and nighttime exploration. Start with a guided kayaking tour through the mangroves of Hurricane Hole, one of the island's most unique ecosystems. Paddle through narrow channels shaded by towering mangrove trees, where the water is so clear you can see the vibrant marine life below. The tranquility of the mangroves, combined with the thrill of exploration, makes this a truly unforgettable experience.

After a day on the water, prepare for an adventure of a different kind—a nighttime exploration of the island's beaches. As the sun sets, head to Salt Pond Bay for a bioluminescent kayaking tour. Paddle through the dark waters, and watch as the water around you lights up with the glow of bioluminescent organisms. Every stroke of your paddle creates a shimmering trail of light, turning the ocean into a magical, glowing wonderland. It's a surreal and breathtaking experience, one that will leave you in awe of the natural wonders that St. John has to offer.

End your day with a bonfire on the beach, sharing stories of your adventures under a sky filled with stars. The warmth of the fire, the sound of the waves, and the company of your fellow adventurers create a perfect ending to your journey—one filled with unforgettable experiences, thrilling challenges, and the joy of discovery.

Day 6: Departure and Reflection

As your adventure-filled journey on St. John comes to an end, take a moment to reflect on the experiences that have shaped your time on the island. The challenges you've overcome, the beauty you've witnessed, and the connections you've made with nature and yourself. The thrill of adventure, the rush of adrenaline, and the serenity of the island's wild places have created memories that will stay with you long after you've left its shores.

As you board the ferry back to St. Thomas, carry with you the spirit of adventure that St. John has awakened in you. The island may be small, but its impact is profound—a place where the call of the wild is answered with every step you take, every wave you ride, and every sunset you witness. St. John is more than a destination for adventurers; it's a place where your spirit is set free, and your soul is forever changed.

Cultural and Historical Itinerary

St. John is not just an island of natural wonders but also a place steeped in rich history and vibrant culture. For those who seek to connect with the soul of the island, a journey through its cultural and historical landmarks offers a deep and meaningful experience. This itinerary is designed for travelers who wish to explore the stories, traditions, and heritage that have shaped St. John, from its ancient roots to its present-day vibrancy.

Day 1: Arrival and Introduction to Cruz Bay

Your cultural journey begins in Cruz Bay, the lively heart of St. John, where the island's past and present converge. After settling into your accommodations, take a leisurely stroll through the town. Visit the Elaine I. Sprauve Library and Museum, housed in a restored plantation great house. Here, you'll find exhibits that trace the island's history, from the indigenous Taino people to the Danish colonial period, offering a fascinating introduction to the cultural tapestry of St. John.

As the evening sets in, immerse yourself in the local culture with a visit to one of the island's music venues. Live performances of reggae, calypso, and quelbe—the traditional folk music of the Virgin Islands—fill the air with the rhythms of the Caribbean. Enjoy a meal at a local restaurant, where you can savor the flavors of the island, from spicy curries to fresh seafood, all infused with a rich blend of cultural influences.

Day 2: Exploring Annaberg Plantation Ruins

On your second day, step back in time with a visit to the Annaberg Plantation Ruins, one of the most significant historical sites on the island. Once a thriving sugar plantation, Annaberg tells the story of the island's colonial past and the enslaved Africans who labored here. As you walk through the stone ruins of the sugar mill, windmill, and factory, you can almost hear the echoes of history—the stories of hardship and resilience that are etched into the very stones of this place.

Take your time exploring the site, reading the interpretive signs that offer insight into the lives of those who lived and worked here. The views from Annaberg are breathtaking, with the turquoise waters of the Caribbean Sea stretching out before you, a stark contrast to the harsh realities of the plantation era. Reflect on the complex history of the island, and honor the strength and spirit of those who endured so much.

In the afternoon, continue your exploration with a visit to the nearby Leinster Bay. This quiet, secluded spot was once a key part of the plantation's operation, where sugar was shipped from the island. Today, it's a peaceful place to walk, swim, or simply sit by the water, letting the history of the island wash over you.

Day 3: Discovering the Indigenous Heritage

Day three is dedicated to exploring the ancient history of St. John, beginning with a hike along the Reef Bay Trail. This trail not only offers a chance to immerse yourself in the island's natural beauty but also leads you to some of its most important archaeological sites. About halfway down the trail, you'll find the famous petroglyphs—mysterious rock carvings made by the Taino people, the island's earliest inhabitants.

These petroglyphs, etched into the rocks beside a freshwater pool, are believed to be over a thousand years old. The carvings, which include faces and symbolic designs, offer a glimpse into the spiritual life of the Taino people. The serene setting, surrounded by lush jungle and the sound of water trickling from the rocks, creates a sense of connection with the past that is both powerful and moving.

After visiting the petroglyphs, continue down the trail to the Reef Bay Sugar Mill Ruins. This site, now engulfed by the jungle, is another testament to the island's complex history. The contrast between the ancient petroglyphs and the colonial ruins offers a unique perspective on the layers of history that have shaped St. John.

Day 4: Coral Bay and Local Traditions

On day four, venture to the quieter side of the island—Coral Bay, a community known for its bohemian spirit and deep connection to the island's traditions. Start your day with a visit to the Emmaus Moravian Church, one of the oldest churches on the island, founded in the 18th century. The church played a crucial role in the lives of the island's enslaved population, offering spiritual support and a sense of community.

From there, explore the small but vibrant local markets and shops in Coral Bay. The artisans here carry on the traditions of the island, creating handmade crafts, jewelry, and art that reflect the culture and beauty of St. John. Take the time to chat with the locals, hear their stories, and learn about the customs and traditions that make this community so unique.

In the afternoon, take part in a traditional West Indian cooking class. Learn how to prepare local dishes such as johnnycakes, saltfish, and fungi, a cornmeal dish similar to polenta. The class offers more than just cooking lessons—it's a window into the island's culinary heritage, passed down through generations.

End your day with a quiet dinner at a local eatery, where you can enjoy the dishes you've learned to prepare, surrounded by the sounds of the island at dusk. The simple, heartfelt flavors of the food, combined with the knowledge you've gained about its cultural significance, create a dining experience that is both nourishing and meaningful.

Day 5: The Legacy of Freedom

Your final full day on St. John is dedicated to exploring the legacy of freedom on the island. Begin with a visit to the Catherineberg Ruins, another former sugar plantation that played a key role in the 1733 slave rebellion, one of the earliest and most significant uprisings in the Caribbean. The ruins are less developed than those at Annaberg, offering a raw, unfiltered glimpse into the island's past.

From Catherineberg, continue to the site of the 1733 Slave Revolt, located near Coral Bay. This site commemorates the brave men and women who fought for their freedom, and it serves as a powerful reminder of the strength and resilience of the island's African ancestors. Reflect on the courage it took to stand up against oppression, and honor the legacy of those who paved the way for future generations.

In the afternoon, visit the Ivan Jadan Museum in Cruz Bay, dedicated to the life and work of the Russian operatic singer who made St. John his home in the mid-20th century. The museum offers a fascinating look at the island's more recent history, highlighting the diverse cultural influences that have shaped its modern identity.

End your day with a quiet walk along the beach, taking in the beauty of the island as the sun sets. The journey through St. John's history and culture may have been filled with stories of struggle and triumph, but it's also a testament to the enduring spirit of the island and its people—a spirit that continues to inspire and uplift all who visit.

Day 6: Departure and Reflection

As your cultural and historical journey on St. John comes to a close, take a moment to reflect on the stories and experiences that have enriched your time on the island. The deep connection to the past, the vibrant traditions, and the warm hospitality of the island's people have left an indelible mark on your heart.

As you board the ferry back to St. Thomas, carry with you the knowledge and appreciation of St. John's rich cultural heritage. The island may be small, but its history is vast, and its culture is alive and thriving. St. John is more than just a beautiful destination; it's a place where the past meets the present, where stories are told, and where the soul of the island is revealed in every step you take.

Chapter 8. Practical Information

Emergency Contacts and Medical Services

When traveling to a place as beautiful and remote as St. John, it's important to be prepared for any unexpected situations. While the island is a paradise of turquoise waters and lush landscapes, emergencies can happen, and knowing where to turn can provide peace of mind and ensure the safety and well-being of your loved ones.

Emergency Contacts

St. John may feel like a world away, but help is always within reach. In case of an emergency, dial 911 for immediate assistance. The operators are trained to handle situations ranging from medical emergencies to fire and police services, and they will guide you through the necessary steps. It's comforting to know that even in this tranquil paradise, you're never truly alone.

For non-urgent medical concerns, you can reach out to the Myrah Keating Smith Community Health Center. Located at Centerline Road, near Cruz Bay, this is the island's primary medical facility, offering a range of services from minor injuries to routine check-ups. The staff is known for their warmth and professionalism, and they understand the unique challenges that come with being on an island. Their phone number is +1 340-693-8900.

For dental emergencies, St. John Dental in Cruz Bay is available. Their number is +1 340-776-2220. Knowing you have access to professional care, even for something as unexpected as a toothache, can make a world of difference.

Medical Services

While St. John doesn't have a full-service hospital, the Myrah Keating Smith Community Health Center is well-equipped for most medical needs. In more serious cases requiring specialized care or surgery, patients are typically transported to St. Thomas via ferry or helicopter. The Schneider Regional Medical Center in St. Thomas is the closest major hospital, offering a comprehensive range of medical services. Their number is +1 340-776-8311.

Pharmacies on the island are also well-stocked with essentials. Cruz Bay Pharmacy in The Marketplace is your go-to for prescription medications, over-the-counter remedies, and general health products. Their phone number is +1 340-776-6880.

While no one expects emergencies, being prepared ensures that your time on the island remains as peaceful and joyful as possible. Whether it's a minor hiccup or a more serious situation, St. John's caring

St john usvi

community and dedicated professionals are there to support you.

Internet and Mobile Connectivity

In the age of constant connectivity, even a remote paradise like St. John ensures you're never too far from the world beyond its shores. Whether you're keeping in touch with loved ones, sharing your adventures on social media, or just wanting the reassurance of being reachable, understanding the island's internet and mobile connectivity can help you stay connected while enjoying your escape.

Internet Connectivity

While St. John invites you to disconnect and immerse yourself in nature, reliable internet access is available across the island. Most hotels, villas, and vacation rentals offer Wi-Fi, allowing you to check emails, upload your stunning beach photos, or stream your favorite shows after a day of exploring. The speeds may vary, but they're generally sufficient for most needs. In Cruz Bay, you'll find several cafes and restaurants offering free Wi-Fi, perfect for a quick connection while sipping a refreshing drink.

For those who need more consistent and faster internet, consider renting a portable Wi-Fi device. This can be a great option if you plan to work remotely or require uninterrupted access during your stay. Keep in mind that in some of the more secluded areas of the island, especially within Virgin Islands National Park, internet access might be limited or slow. But perhaps that's just nature's way of encouraging you to fully embrace the island's tranquility.

Mobile Connectivity

St. John is part of the U.S. Virgin Islands, so if you're traveling from the U.S., your mobile phone should work seamlessly here. Most major U.S. carriers provide coverage on the island, though service can be spotty in more remote areas. Before you arrive, it's wise to check with your provider about your plan's coverage and any potential roaming charges.

For international visitors, purchasing a local SIM card upon arrival is a good option. This ensures you have local coverage at a reasonable cost, allowing you to stay connected without worry.

As you bask in the island's beauty, knowing that the digital world is just a tap away can provide a comforting balance between adventure and connection.

Tipping and Service Charges

In the warm embrace of St. John, where hospitality is as abundant as the island's natural beauty, tipping is more than just a customary practice—it's a way to express gratitude for the kindness and care you'll undoubtedly receive. As you enjoy the island's vibrant

St john usvi

dining scene, embark on thrilling adventures, or simply relax in the comfort of your accommodation, understanding the local tipping customs will ensure you show your appreciation in the way that's expected.

Restaurants and Bars

When dining out in St. John, tipping follows the same general guidelines as in the mainland United States. A standard tip of 15-20% of the total bill is customary for good service in restaurants. If the service goes above and beyond, you may wish to tip more, reflecting the island's spirit of generosity and appreciation. In some establishments, particularly those catering to tourists, a service charge might already be included in the bill—typically around 18%. It's always a good idea to check your bill before tipping, just to ensure you're not tipping twice.

At bars, it's customary to tip $1 to $2 per drink, or about 15-20% of the total tab if you're settling at the end of the night. Whether you're enjoying a craft cocktail by the beach or a local rum punch, your tip is a small way to thank the bartender for their skill and service.

Taxis and Tours

For taxi rides, a tip of 10-15% of the fare is typical, though it's also common to round up to the nearest dollar. If a driver assists with luggage or provides helpful tips and information about the island, consider tipping a bit more. When participating in guided tours, a tip of 15-20% of the tour cost is customary, particularly if your guide has gone out of their way to make your experience memorable.

Accommodations

When staying in hotels or vacation rentals, tipping the housekeeping staff is a thoughtful gesture. Leaving a few dollars per day, or a larger tip at the end of your stay, shows appreciation for the care taken to keep

St john usvi

your space clean and comfortable. If a concierge or other staff member provides exceptional service, a small tip can go a long way in showing your gratitude.

Tipping on St. John is a way to give back to the community that will welcome you so warmly, ensuring that your stay is not just enjoyable, but heartwarming as well.

Conclusion

As your journey through the pages of this guide comes to a close, we hope your anticipation for St. John's breathtaking beauty has only grown. From the serene beaches of Trunk Bay to the rich history of Annaberg Plantation, and the vibrant local culture, this island is a treasure trove of experiences waiting to be discovered. Whether you're seeking adventure in its turquoise waters, relaxation under its swaying palms, or a deeper connection with its heritage, St. John offers something truly special for every traveler.

As you step onto its sun-kissed shores, may this guide serve as your companion, helping you navigate the island's hidden gems and well-known wonders alike. Let its insights enhance your journey, turning moments into memories and encounters into cherished stories.

We've poured our hearts into creating this guide with the hope that it enriches your time on St. John, making your stay as magical and fulfilling as the island itself. Your feedback means the world to us, and we'd love to hear about your experiences and how this guidebook has been a part of your adventure. Please consider leaving a review—your thoughts not only help us improve but also assist future travelers in making the most of their own St. John journeys.

Thank you for choosing this guide as your travel companion. Here's to an unforgettable adventure on the beautiful island of St. John!

Made in the USA
Middletown, DE
25 August 2024

59681216R00086